Welc[illegible] Tae'

- The Covid Years

Short inspirational stories with a moment in the Word!

Nigel E. Gill

Dedication

This Book is dedicated to my Lord and Saviour Jesus Christ from whom all blessings flow.

Acknowledgement

I wish to thank all who encouraged and motivated me to make this possible. Without you this would never have become a reality for it was never my dream.

Contents

Foreward

We really enjoyed proof-reading 'An cupán tae with the Rev, the Covid years' Just to let you know, the phrase 'an cupán tae' is an Irish one and is pronounced 'on cup-on tay' and simply means a cup of tea. In Ireland many a topic or issue is discussed or resolved over the medium of a cup of tea, and in essence, that is the character or nature of this book. It is one to be enjoyed over a cup of your favourite brew.

This book is full of encouragement, warmth, good humour and doses of gentle challenge. It reminded us of our Lord Jesus as He spoke in parables to the shepherds and fishermen. He understood His audience and spoke in simple language using examples that everyone could identify with. That's exactly what Nigel does in this book. It is utterly disarming and absolutely accessible to all. You will be blessed.

'An cupán tae with the Rev' started life as a weekly video chat Nigel used to have with his parishioners during Covid 19. It gained such popularity that its admirers felt it should be published to reach a wider audience. We have no doubt that you will find your love for God greatly enhanced by the nuggets of revelation that Nigel extracts from everyday experiences allied to relevant Scriptures. Thank you Nigel for your openness to the Lord and for all the insights you share.

Norman and Joan Simpson.

October 16th 2020

Time for "An Cupán Tae" with the Rev!

Hi folks!

Welcome to 'an cupán tae with the Rev!' See that was one of the things that I used to say at work, you know –'it's time to stick the kettle on' or 'let's go and get our 'cupán tae,' and that meant that you sat down and had your cup of tea, and you ended up having a chat for a few minutes about all sorts of things.

This is something that really struck me today. As a result I'm going to start this little 'an cupán tae with the Rev!' so that you and I can chat about a whole variety of things. At work we used to talk about everything! I mean EVERYTHING! I'm hoping we can do the same here.

As I worked in a Tyre Shop, frequent conversations were about Car SOS, Ice Road Truckers, Soccer, Formula One, and Kildare Football. Being an Offaly man, Kildare football was always great for a bit of banter with the lads. Even though Offaly football was every bit as bad as

Kildare football, you could at least get a bit of craic out of it!

Of course, there were obviously loads of times when we would chat about God. The guys all knew that I was involved in church and church stuff and so they would ask me what I did at the weekend. What "masses" did I take? How many were there? What was I speaking on? All these kinds of conversations used to come up. So, I would just like to encourage you for a moment over our 'an cupán tae' together.

I would like to read to you from Deuteronomy 6:4-12. This was God's word to the people of Israel:

> Hear, O Israel: The Lord our God, the Lord is one. Love the Lord your God with all your heart and with all your soul and with all your strength. These commandments that I give you today are to be on your hearts. Impress them on your children. Talk about them when you sit at home and when you walk along the road, when you lie down and when you get up. Tie them as symbols on your hands and

> bind them on your foreheads. Write them on the doorframes of your houses and on your gates. When the Lord your God brings you into the land He swore to your fathers, to Abraham, Isaac and Jacob, to give you a land with large, flourishing cities you didn't build, houses filled with all kinds of good things you didn't provide, wells you didn't dig, and vineyards and olive groves you didn't plant, then when you eat and are satisfied, be careful that you don't forget the Lord, who brought you out of Egypt, out of the land of slavery.

But the thing I just want to focus on today is: Yes, we're in a lockdown. Yes, we have restrictions upon our lives right now. But God is still the same! Have you been talking to Him about the lockdown and Covid 19? What has God said about these issues. Have you shared your thoughts with God? Or even with your friends? Who did you talk to God about and did you tell your friends what God means to you?

This scripture goes and says that we are to impress the commandments on our children. We are to talk about God at home. We are to talk about Him as we go for our five kilometre walk. We are to be people who simply end up just "oozing" Jesus, talking about His goodness to us.

So let me ask you a question: Are your eyes on Jesus right now or on COVID-19?[1] Are you wondering where God is? Maybe you have stopped talking about God? Maybe it's time for an oul' cup of tea? Maybe it's time for a chat? Maybe it's time for that five kilometre walk believing that God is going to have you meet someone you can talk to about Him. Maybe it's time to make a phone call or send a text message? What's your conversation about today? – "Oh how I wish life was better!" or is it filled with the goodness of God? Let me leave that with you.

---

[1] Or whatever circumstance you are in at time of reading!

October 22nd 2020

Taste and See!

Greetings People! Welcome to this week's 'an cupán tae with the Rev'. Today I want to look at this little verse which has been on my mind for a few weeks now, and it is "Taste and see that the Lord is good." It is found in Psalm 34 and verse 8. But just to give you the context, I shall read part of the Psalm to you. Psalm 34:1-8:

> I will extol the Lord at all times. His praise will always be on my lips. My soul will boast in the Lord and the afflicted will hear and rejoice. Glorify the Lord with me. Let us exalt His name together. I sought the Lord and He answered me. He delivered me from all my fears. Those who look to Him are radiant. Their faces are never covered with shame. This poor man called and the Lord heard him. He saved him out of all his troubles. The angel of the Lord encamps around those who fear Him and He

delivers them. I will taste and see that the Lord is good. Blessed is the man who takes refuge in Him.

When I think of the words 'taste and see', the image that comes to my mind is of when I was young. My mother would often say: 'Stop eating with your eyes!', 'That food is good for you!' or 'Get it into you!' But when it came to lettuce and tomatoes and cabbage and whatever, no matter how many times I looked at it or even tasted it, it was just like – BLAAAAHHH!

But what the Psalmist is telling us here is, the Lord is good. That's it. It's a statement, a factual statement that he makes. Yes, in the context of the Psalm he goes and shares with us what God had done for him and what God can do for you. Isn't it a lovely verse as we face lockdown yet again? 'I sought the Lord and He answered me. He delivered me from all my fears.' This is why the Psalmist goes and says that the Lord is good. What are your fears today?

For me, one of the reasons why the Lord is good is that He says 'taste and see'. So often, because we tend just to taste things with our eyes we don't realise there's more to tasting a thing than that! One of my favourite snacks is a grapefruit. Now the thing about a grapefruit is, it can be quite bitter to taste, but I love it. I love the taste of it!

But very often as I said we do eat with our eyes. Very often we do look at food exactly the same way my mother was trying to stop us looking at it. With taste comes a decision. You have to decide that you are going to commit yourself to eating this, to tasting that. And that is when we discover that there are things that we taste that we like and really enjoy. And so it is when it comes to this scripture.

What the Psalmist is saying is 'taste and see' that the Lord is good but it's only in tasting that we will actually see that the Lord is good. It's only in committing ourselves to doing that, that we'll discover that the Lord is good. It's only in seeking Him that we'll know that the Lord is good.

Back in the Garden of Eden, Satan came along in the form of the serpent to Adam and Eve as you all know. But what came next? Genesis tells us that 'when Eve looked at the fruit, she saw it was good for food.' That is the natural way we consider food, but here in the Psalm it is the reverse. The Psalmist is saying 'taste and see' that the Lord is good. What do you need to do to 'taste and see' that the Lord is good? You have to commit to tasting it.

You see a decision is needed with my grapefruit. I need to commit myself to taking the skin off it, opening it up, taking a piece and placing it in my mouth. Then I can enjoy its flavour. That is what God is asking of you. Commit to the process. Let us 'taste and see' that the Lord is good. Enjoy your natural food and the spiritual food that God provides this week. Taste and see that the Lord is good.

October 29th 2020

Happy is the One…

How's it goin'? Welcome to this week's 'cupán tae with the Rev'. It's good to see you looking so well and I trust this finds you feeling well. The verse of scripture I want to think about today, while we're having our 'cupán tae,' is actually the continuation of last week's verse which was Psalm 34:8:

> Taste and see that the Lord is good. Blessed is the man who takes refuge in Him.

So last week we considered 'taste and see' that the Lord is good. This week I want to consider the second part: Blessed is the person, the man, the woman, the child who takes refuge in Him.

One of the things I find interesting is how family can be very subtle about the way they go and talk to you about things! Do you know what I mean? For example, I was given this mug…

NOT A MORNING PERSON

DOESN'T BEGIN TO COVER IT.

Not nice! I tell you, not nice! I was also given this mug: Mr. Grumpy. But today I'm talking about happiness. And maybe the best person to talk about happiness is someone who is Mr. Grumpy!

On an occasion long past I had this form from one of the churches I used to go to. It was to help you define your gifts and your abilities, your strengths and weaknesses. As I was working in the Tyre Shop, I decided in my madness to give it to the receptionist there. She said all sorts of lovely things about me. And then she went and said: “when under pressure, tends towards grumpiness!’ So maybe the best person to talk about happiness is someone who is grumpy!

This verse of scripture uses the word ‘Blessed’ and those who are very caught up in sacred words will be upset with me now. But blessed actually means happy. Happy is the one who takes refuge in the Lord. And so here we are in the middle of our pandemic and we're in our second week of lockdown. The government and the World Health

Organization and NPHED[2] are all speaking about the whole person and they mention our mental wellbeing, physical wellbeing, emotional wellbeing, but they never mention our spiritual wellbeing!

And one of the things that really struck me is that in the last pages of this book, the Bible, which was completed nearly 2000 years ago, there are many references to happiness, and if we translate the word blessed, it does actually mean happy. Happy is the person who finds refuge in Him!

Now let me talk about that. It's spilling rain! It's spilling rain today, It was spilling rain yesterday. And if you're out walking in the rain, you know this scene well. If you're walking in the rain and you end up standing in a shed... outside that shed the circumstances haven't changed! It's still raining, it's still pouring cats and dogs, but you are sheltered. And that's what the word refuge means. God is our shelter, our refuge from the storm.

So let me ask you something today. The storm is what the storm is! The pandemic is what the pandemic is! The

---

2 NPHED: National Public Health Emergency Team

circumstances you find yourself in are the circumstances in which you find yourself! But is God your shelter? Is God someone in whom you can find refuge? Because the truth is, just as you enjoy standing in the shed looking out at the rain falling outside, knowing that you are dry, in that same way in the circumstances of life, the Psalmist is telling us that Happy… Blessed… is the person who finds refuge in the Lord. I hope you can say with me that that's who God is for you.

So 'till next time, enjoy your 'cupán tae.' After all, blessed is the one who finds refuge in the Lord. Happy is the one who finds refuge in the Lord! Now, that surely is a reason for us to sing about even in the rain!

November 5th 2020

Mind Your Mood…

Well how are Ya? Oh, there's the kettle now. I need a tea bag. Some hot water. How are you? Welcome to 'an cupán tae with the Rev'. So what are you having? I'm afraid, all I have now is a bit of green tea here. And as for milk and sugar, I don't use milk. And with regard to sugar, I think I'm sweet enough already! I don't know whether you'd agree or not, but there you go. There's the old tea ready now. Perfect job. Ahhhhhh… that's good, if I say so meself!

Anyway, this week I was just thinking as I was listening to the radio about the phrase, 'mind your mood' which was being used in an ad. about your mental health in regard to the times we're living in.... MIND YOUR MOOD, hmmm!

And as I was sitting there I was wondering what sort of mood I was supposed to mind? I didn't really know what it was all about. So I decided to look it up. And of course, it's all about mental well-being, etc. etc. But as I was thinking about the phrase 'mind your mood', the first prescription to help mind your mood that came to my mind is from 1 Thessalonians 5:16-18. And it reads:

> Be joyful always. Pray continually, give thanks in all circumstances for this is God's will for you in Christ Jesus.

Regarding, 'give thanks in all circumstances,' I would consider myself a very thankful person, a very grateful person. But when it comes to actually expressing it, I'd say I'm very poor. Very poor about going and saying thank you. Thank you for anything for that matter.

I was staying with a couple a long time ago and at every meal time this man turned around and thanked his wife for the food that was on the table. In fact, he was a very humble, gracious man when I come to think about it. And maybe you could say he was practising the attitude of gratitude. But I have to confess I am not a bit like that. There is room for improvement!

Now, I've been pondering as you know, about giving thanks in all circumstances, even when times are hard -

that can be difficult. I'm not going to say it isn't difficult. It is difficult to give thanks in all circumstances!

However, as I was thinking about this, do you know what came to mind? I thought about Maslow and Maslow's hierarchy of needs. Actually I'm not a person who's big into psychology, to be honest. I just think it's head-wrecking material! But as I said I was thinking, what is the common denominator in which we can all have something to be grateful for?

Maslow, in his hierarchy of needs, says the basic physiological needs that we all have are food, water, warmth and rest.

Food! Water, Warmth and Rest!

So today, if you're thinking about what you have to be thankful for, and you want a place to start giving thanks, maybe that's a good place to start!

However, if things aren't going well, say if you've lost your job, or maybe you're not sure how you'll be able to make ends meet, or maybe you're concerned about your child living away from home, or maybe you're concerned about the exams your children will be doing this year, so much for food, water, warmth and rest! Maybe I don't know what your maybe is, lots of maybes, maybe you've got bad news about health, maybe you're really wondering how you're going to cope….!

And here I am sharing a scripture that has been on my mind about 'giving thanks in all circumstances for this is the will of God in Christ Jesus concerning you'. Maybe a good place for us to start off is by giving thanks for what we do have! What if we stopped up[3] and thanked God that we actually do have food, thanked God that we do have water, thanked God that we do have somewhere warm to stay, thanked God that we can stop up and rest, and start from that space.

So what am I thankful for? Well I'm thankful for all those things, I'm thankful for my 'cupán tae,' I'm thankful that I can communicate with you and that we can stop up and have this chat together over our 'cupán tae.' I'm also very

---

[3]"Stopped up" – a colloquialism meaning: 'to pause, to take time out to reflect, to stop and think or chat'. The meaning is based on when a farmer stops his tractor for a chat with someone else. The only way a conversation could happen was by having 'to stop up'.

thankful for the dry day outside, thankful that the rain has stopped. Thankful that I'm alive and well. Thankful that with every breath I have there is hope, there's a reason to live! I'm thankful that the reason I'm living is God. God has given me a reason to live! God has a purpose for my life no matter what the circumstances.

If God wants us to be a thankful people, maybe begin by expressing a little bit of thanks today. What have you got to be thankful for? Let's just think about that, while we're having our 'cupán tae.

November 12th 2020

Take a Break!

Well Hello, Hello, Hello and welcome to this week's 'an cupán tae with the Rev.' You know, the problem with this lockdown and working from home is that one day rolls into another. You end up forgetting what day of the week you're in!

Well, I ended up being challenged by a fellow minister about Sabbath rest the other day. Sabbath rest? Okay, sure we know what that really means biblically: The Lord went and created the world in six days and on the seventh day He rested. So what are you doing about taking a rest, Nigel? That was the question he was asking. Well, I'll just tell you a little story…

Last Sunday morning I had listened to the radio show, and then I sent out my Sunday service via social media to everyone as the church buildings were closed due to the lockdown. After that I went down to feed my cattle, and on my way home from looking at the cattle, I met the postman! And I tell you one thing, he frightened the life out of me. I seriously thought I'd missed a day. I was like, oh my goodness. I've sent out my Sunday service on Monday!

But what's the postman doing here? Now apparently he's being overrun with parcels. The postal business is very busy because of lockdown and so we got to having a chat about it. And as I was thinking about that, I realised you know, how easy it is for one day just to roll into another, that our sense of structure is gone. So that got me thinking about the scripture in Matthew 11:28 -30 where Jesus said:

> "Come to me, all you who are weary and burdened, and I will give you rest. Take my yoke upon you and learn from me, for I am gentle and humble in heart, and you will find rest for your souls. For my yoke is easy and my burden is light."

You know, it struck me that for many people at this present moment, lockdown is a burden. This is something that is weighing them down. This is something because it's so abnormal, and being cut off and shut away from people is undoubtedly something difficult. And I'm not immune to that.

In fact, I felt a bit like one of those individuals left behind in an apocalyptic novel or film waking to discover that you're all alone, isolated, cut off from the world and the only way to communicate is through your laptop!

And the reality is that people, not only me, but people, that's where they're at, they're feeling isolated, cut off, alone. One day rolls into another. And the thing that concerns me is our need and possible neglect of spiritual rest. You know, it was a very good challenge that was put to me: what do I do about spiritual rest? What do you do in regard to your soul? In regard to your whole overall spiritual well-being? Jesus goes and says, "Come unto me, all you who are weary and heavy-laden, and I will give you rest!"

We've been encouraged to go and maintain relationships and keep in touch with people. But for the goodness of our soul, Jesus says, "Come. Let's have a conversation". Now let me ask you a question: When is the last time that you and Jesus took a break together? When did you and Jesus have an oul' 'cupán tae?' Jesus says, "come unto me, all you who are weary, worn down, tired, burdened and heavy-laden, and I will give you rest."

So maybe we need to take Jesus up on His offer in the midst of the craziness we find ourselves in. Yes, maybe it is that we need to take a moment, to come aside and rest. Let the world just be what it is. Let the craziness be what the craziness is. And just sit down and have a few moments… just you and Jesus. After all, He's inviting you. Let's just leave it there. Have a blessed day!

November 18th 2020

Keep in Step!

Ah, there you are! How are you? Welcome to 'an cupán tae with the Rev!' As you can see I was just reading the paper. And as you can also see, I also had a fight with the lawnmower,[4] and the lawnmower won! I came out second best.

In the paper I was reading about these two ladies and they have started up an Instagram site called 'Keeping Up with The Hastings'. And if you want to know all about grass growth and how to go and get your cattle finishing and all that sort of stuff, just follow them on Instagram. And you know what, that got me thinking. It got me thinking about the way things were when I was growing up. People used to always be talking about keeping up with the Joneses. I haven't a clue who the Joneses were. No idea at all who the Joneses might be. And now we're all aware of the TV programmes encouraging you about

---

[4] "Had a fight with a lawnmower" is a colloquialism meaning: you got a haircut!

keeping up with this or that person – social influencers they call them. Well, I'll tell you one thing. Fair dues if you can keep up with them because you'd want to have some budget! But anyway, that's all neither here nor there, but it got me thinking…

We spend our lives trying to keep up with things. And the scripture that came to my mind was Galatians 5:25 where it tells us:

> Since we live by the Spirit…
>
> let us keep in step with the Spirit.

Hmmm… since we live by the Spirit, let us keep in step with the Spirit. And you know, I'm just thinking, God isn't asking us to keep up! It isn't that we have to be somehow exerting energy to always be in that space, or the player at the front as the trailblazer, or to be the person who's making waves. No, no, no, it's not about that at all!

We have to keep in step with the Spirit. And if anything, what this pandemic should have been telling us or showing us is just how our life seems like a rat race in which we're always running and trying to make ends meet, trying to keep up and put on a lifestyle that maybe we can't really afford. Always trying to be one step ahead. Always trying to be in front of the posse. And God is saying, keep in step with the Spirit!

Now, as you know by the size of me, I am someone that would find it very hard to keep up with anything anyway! And so when I was thinking about this, I wondered what it means to keep in step with the Spirit?

Considering the rat race of life, when you're rushing and racing, there are all sorts of emotions that manifest such as anger, frustration, infuriation, all these things. It isn't that God is asking us to slow down and come to a stop. It isn't that God is asking us to be rushing and racing. It isn't that God is saying, be part of the rat race.

What God is saying to us is keep in step with the Spirit. Keeping in step with the Spirit means that God wants us to be a people of love, joy, peace, patience, gentleness, self-control and faithfulness.

I don't think the Fruit of the Spirit is something that is off in the future, or something that can be achieved by rushing and racing!

And if Covid-19 has done anything, if this lockdown has

done anything, it should be that we have had to press the reset button, to consider what is important to us.

As for me, I think to keep in step with the Spirit means to be someone who's moving at a pace where the fruits of the Spirit, love, joy, peace, patience, kindness, goodness, faithfulness and self-control are evident in my life. What do you think?

November 25th 2020

I've Got the Joy, Joy, Joy, Joy…

Ah! How are you? Welcome to 'an cupán tae with the Rev!' I was just thinking there of a children's chorus; it's been in my mind for the last few days:

> I've got the joy, joy, joy, joy down in my heart, down in my heart, down in my heart.
> I've got the joy, joy, joy, joy down in my heart, down in my heart to stay.[5]

Now some people will go and say that the joy is that far pressed down in my heart, that it's got no other choice but to stay! But I've been thinking this week, ruminating. You know, to ruminate means to chew on it, to be like a cow who is chewing the cud, you know. Thinking it over,

---

[5] Quotation taken from the chorus by GW Cook: I've got the joy joy, joy, joy.

mulling it over, ruminating. I've been ruminating on this scripture in James 1:2 to:

> Consider it pure joy, my brothers and sisters, whenever you face trials of many kinds.

Now there's more to the verse than that, which I'll get into in a moment. It concerns the notion of considering it pure joy when you face many trials, or trials of many kinds.

Due to the effects of the Covid 19 pandemic there are businesses wondering if they're going to open or not, and there are churches wondering if they're going to open and some are saying, "Oh, we must open!" because of the season that's in it and all the rest of it.

Personally, I'd like it if the church was opened. But when I reflect back, when I ruminate on the last number of weeks and the challenges lockdown has created, I ask myself the question, 'did I consider this pure joy?' And the answer truthfully, I would think, is no. And yet here's James in his epistle writing to the believers of the time in James 1:3 and he's saying:

> Consider it pure joy my brothers and sisters, whenever you face trials of many kinds.

Now I checked it out: this "Pure joy." That joy that he's actually speaking of is only a joy that can be found in God. Actually the root word for that sort of joy is the same as grace. It's a joy that has its foundation, its source in the grace of God. And so the only way that we can have that joy is by being in a relationship with God and having an understanding of things from God's perspective.

And that's what brings us into the second part of the verse. Consider it pure joy my brothers and sisters, whenever you face trials of many kinds:

> because you know that the testing of your faith produces perseverance.

So let me ask you something. Has this time been a testing of your faith? Has it been a time where you are actually being tested by God? What has God revealed to you of your faith in this last 10 weeks of lockdown? What has

God revealed to you in this last 10 weeks of not being able to have social interaction the way we usually do? What has God revealed to you through the fact that you've maybe had to be cocooning, or perhaps your business hasn't been going well, or that you may have lost your job, or that church doesn't function as church should, or that you can't meet family the way you'd love to as normal, or that you can't socialize with your friends?

Consider it pure joy when you have faced many trials or trials of many kinds. Why? Because you know that the testing of your faith produces perseverance. But that brings us to another question, doesn't it? That brings us to the question: Where is your faith? What is your faith based on? Maybe we'll spend some time ruminating on that one. So until the next time. God bless.

December 2nd 2020

A Cheerful Heart is…

Hey! welcome to 'an cupán tae with the Rev!' You see one of the things that has been striking me recently is the number of people who are all the time asking me about my mental well-being. As if there's something wrong with me. I mean, come on!

I went to ask a friend if he'd do a little thing for me on the radio. And he replies with: "Nigel, how are you?" almost implying that there was a problem because I'd asked him to do something! There's something wrong with my mental well-being just because I asked him to come on the radio!

But that got me thinking about the whole topic of self-medication. Now I'm wondering when they're talking about my mental state if they think I might need some sort of medication, and if so, are they talking about me having a drink or drugs (prescribed of course) or who knows what else to sustain me or to keep me going?

But all that train of thought did was get me thinking about

scripture and I landed into Romans chapter 12:2 where Paul says:

> Do not conform any longer to the pattern of this world but be transformed in the renewing of your mind.

We are to do this in the light of God's mercy. Then I got thinking about medication and Proverbs 17:22 declares:

> A cheerful heart is good medicine but a crushed spirit dries up the bones.

Let me ask you a question. Right now be honest with me. Are you someone who has got a crushed spirit or a cheerful heart? When I come into the house the odd time, I might be grinning from ear to ear about something and do you know what, Herself, Queen Victoria, turns around and says, "So what has you so happy?" As if it's outside the norm for me to be happy, like!

A cheerful heart is good medicine. So how do I medicate my mind? Well if we look at what Paul was saying to medicate your mind, you would need to look at life in the light of God's mercy. I need to look at my life in the light of God's mercy!

And when I stop up to do that, I think about all God's goodness to me. I think about all His blessings to me and five minutes isn't going to cover just what He has done for me! The old hymn says:

> Count your blessings, name them one by one,
> and it will surprise you what the Lord has done.[6]

So while you're finishing your old 'cupán tae,' count your blessings. Proverbs 17:22 states: "A cheerful heart is good medicine!" Let us medicate our minds in the light of God's mercy, the wonders of his blessings and the fulfilment of his promises to us. At a time, such as this, isn't the greatest promise of all… God is with us! What did Jesus say?

---

[6] Quotation taken from the hymn by Johnson Oatmans: When upon life's billows you are tempest tossed.

'I will never leave you or forsake you.' Now that is something to be excited about. Have a great week with the Holy Spirit.

December 9th 2020

Overflowing with Hope…

Níl aon tinteán le do thinteán féin, there's no fireplace like your own fireplace! Welcome to this week's 'an cupán tae with the Rev'. As you can see I've got into the old festive spirit here, now, today. As we are approaching Christmas, the thing that's on my mind is hope. Some people find this a very hopeless time of year, they find it a hard time. But that's because, I would say, we place our hope in the wrong sort of things. The old hymn goes and says:

My hope is built on nothing less
Than Jesus' blood and righteousness.
I dare not trust the sweetest frame,
But wholly lean on Jesus name,
On Christ the solid rock I stand,
All other ground is sinking the sand.[7]

---

[7] Quotation taken from the Hymn by E. Mote - My hope is built on nothing less

And that is what Christmas is all about. Christmas is about the fact that Christ came and that Christ is our hope. And that got me thinking about what Paul went and wrote to the Romans, just at the very end of his book. He wrote this little blessing and I want to share it with you. In Romans 15:13 he writes:

> May the God of hope fill you with all joy and peace as you trust in him so that you may overflow with hope by the power of the Holy Spirit.

I'm going to read that again: May the God of hope fill you with all joy and peace as you trust in him so that you may overflow with hope by the power of the Holy Spirit. Do you know what I like about that verse? It goes and tells us that God is the source of our hope. God is hope. Our God is THE God of hope.

It is God who is the one who gives us hope and that excites me because it isn't something of myself. It isn't something that I need to find in things. It hasn't got to do with the people around me. It's outside of that whole sphere. It is God Himself who is the God of hope. It is

God Himself who is the one who gives me hope and that is exciting…

But Paul goes on and prays, May the God of hope fill you with all joy and peace. Now we get Christmas cards coming at this time of year which say 'Joy' or 'Peace' on the front of them. The reason that we have those words written on Christmas cards is because Jesus Christ has come and we have these things through Him. We have that hope through Him. We have that peace through Him. We have that joy through Him.

So rather than looking for hope in it being a perfect Christmas, or hope in things working out the way we would like them to, or hope that we'd actually end up being with family, or hope that this vaccine is going to take away the virus that's lurking around us, let's rejoice in the hope we have in God. Remember, Paul says, 'May the God of hope fill you with all joy and peace.'

But the next phrase of the verse states "as you trust in Him", so there's something we can do! We are to trust in God, but note what happens as you trust in Him. This is what happens…'so that you may overflow with hope by the power of the Holy Spirit.'

So think about that as the God of hope goes and fills us with joy and peace and our lives overflow. It isn't just that it's going to be a little more hope, or a little measure of hope. It isn't that there's just going to be a little glimmer of hope. It isn't that there's something like a silver lining or all those other sorts of phrases about hope. Oh, no, we are going to overflow with hope. Through the power of the Holy Spirit. That is my prayer for you this Christmas. May the God of hope fill you with all joy and peace as you trust in Him that you may overflow with hope in the power of the Holy Spirit.

So have a blessed, happy, joy-filled, peaceful, overflowing Christmas, filled with hope. OVERFLOWING WITH HOPE. So until next time thank you for joining me for this 'cupán tae.

December 17th 2020

Filled to the Measure…

Oh, how are you? Folks, you know it's Christmas, when the RTE Christmas guide is out in the shops. Now for this 'cupán tae' I have my Christmas mug! The other thing is that the children have almost started a tradition in our house – they have us listening to some Christmas station. And so when I got into the car this morning to head off to get a few bits and pieces like meal for my cattle, and switched on the ignition, BOOM, BOOM, BOOM! - Christmas music was blaring through the speakers and I was afflicted with Christmas songs. Songs I never even heard of!

But one of the things that really struck me about these Christmas songs is, goodness me, there are plenty of issues of a psychological nature lurking there. It's unbelievable. I mean, there are songs all about self-preservation. There are songs asking good old St. Nicolaus himself for all sorts of things. I tell you, with the list of demands there, a fellow would want to be careful about who he would marry because there are some right gold-diggers out there looking for cars, yachts, all sorts of crazy things. And then there are the songs overflowing with emotional issues; you would be broke paying for a psychiatrist or a psychologist or both! Seriously, check them out for yourself.

And if that's what Christmas is all about, then there's a problem. For me, Christmas is about Christ. Christmas is about His coming and His birth. And the thing I would like to share with you is this, Paul's prayer from Ephesians chapter 3. You see this is what I would like for you for Christmas.

But before I say that, it's good to see you and see you looking so good and a belated welcome to our 'an cupán tae with the Rev!' Now, as I said, Paul writes in Ephesians 3: 16-19 his prayer, and it's my prayer for you. Let's listen to his words:

> I pray that out of His (God's) glorious, riches, He may strengthen you with power through His Spirit in your inner being. So that Christ may dwell in your hearts through faith. And I pray that you, being rooted and established in love, may have power together with all the saints to grasp

> how wide and long and deep is the love of Christ. And to know this love that surpasses knowledge, that you may be filled to the measure of all the fullness of God.

Filled to the measure of all the fullness of God! When we think about this year, it's been tough, but I love that saying, you know, to grasp how wide, high, long and deep is the love of God. It reminds me of a cat soaking up the sun.

Did you ever see a cat that is stretched out soaking up the sun? Now you won't see a cat stretched out at this time of year with it being so miserable and cold out there. But when you see a cat in the summer and it's lying there, just soaking up the sun; well my prayer is that this Christmas time, you are going to be so aware of the love of Christ that you're going to be like that cat! Just as it soaks up the sun, my prayer is that you will be soaking in the love of God.

The reason for this prayer is this folks: just imagine this reality that says that you are going to be filled with that love which surpasses knowledge and that you are going to be filled to the measure of the fullness of God! Now you see, it's not about you! You are not the measure. No! it is to the measure of the fullness of God! Just imagine it…

Last week we talked about overflowing, but the thing is, this week our prayer is that you and I are filled to the fullness of the measure of God. So it is all of God! It is all about His love and Paul is praying that you would be filled and also have a knowledge of this reality, and he is praying that this love will be put into you. I mean, how can you not be excited about that? Think about it! This Christmas, if God, the creator of the universe, the creator of our world were to indwell your innermost being, your innermost being would be filled to the measure of the fullness of God! Wow! How? It says here by the power of the Spirit.

Now the Greek word for the phrase 'by the power of' here is 'Dunamis' which is the word which was taken to describe the power contained within dynamite. Dynamite is our closest definition, or way of understanding the raw power contained in this passage! Just imagine folks, just imagine that you are being filled with the love of God to such a point that all you can do is EXPLODE! All you can do is explode with the love that God has given you.

Oh, that's my prayer for you this Christmas, that you will be so in tune with the love of God, that all it can do is radiate out through every pore of your being!

We have a little poster up outside our church that says: 'Christmas is a time to reflect.' So often I think about that as I look inward and think about the year that's just passed. But no, no, maybe we are like the baubles on the Christmas tree. They are just glowing, reflecting the light that shines upon them. Or maybe, just as the moon reflects the sun's light upon us, so it is that we ought to reflect Christ's love. So let us also reflect His love onto every person, every area, every facet of our society. I'm praying as I drink this week's little 'cupán tae' with you, that this Christmas, God is going to fill you up by His power through the Spirit with the love of Christ so that you may get to know that love and you will be filled to the measure of the fullness of God. Have a Happy Christmas in Jesus' name, Amen!

January 7th 2021

The New Year is looking Good!

My happy soul rejoices,
the sky is bright above.
I'll join the Heavenly voices,
and sing redeeming love[8]…

Whoa! Well, how's it going and a Happy New Year to you! Welcome to our 'an cupán tae with the Rev.' But Folks, I can't get that song out of my head, my happy soul rejoices, the sky is bright above. I'll join the heavenly voices and sing redeeming love.

Now as you can see, there is a small change of location. I'm working here now; on a little log cabin that I got, which I'm turning into my office. I've been evicted from the house because, well, to be honest, my wife, Queen Victoria, keeps the house beautifully and I'm the source of

---

[8] Quotation taken from the Hymn by Fanny Crosby – My happy soul rejoices

the clutter. So, I have my own space now. I've got to get all my books and stuff out of the house and let her get her house back to normal.

You know, I can't help it, but I'm buzzing. I'm so excited. I'm excited about this New Year. Ah, sure, who cares that Santa Claus came along and delivered presents and at the same time ended up shutting the whole country down with yet another lockdown while delivering our Christmas presents. Who cares? Here's the thing: It's important that we do as we should do, but we all have a reason to be here and that excites me. I have to tell you my God is just amazing. There's stuff that is just floating in my brain and I'm excited about this New Year.

I don't know about you, but I'm excited about us and here's why I'm excited about us. Oh, here we are, in Acts 17:25, it says this:

> And God is not served by human hands as if He needed anything since He Himself, gives to all new life and breath and everything else. From one man, He made every nation of men that they should

> inhabit the whole earth, and He determined the times set for them and the exact places where they should live.

Now think about that. God has determined the times that you're supposed to live. The exact times and the exact place where you should live. Do you know what that means? I'll tell you what that means. That means that COVID-19 is not going to dictate my days. That means that cancer is not going to dictate my days. Now it doesn't mean that I won't get COVID-19 or that I may not get cancer. That's a different argument.

But what I'm saying is that my days are in God's hands. Your days are in God's hands. So my happy soul rejoices, the sky is bright above. And I'll join the heavenly voices and sing redeeming love! Why? For there's power in Jesus' blood. And do you know what; this is a year that God intended that you and I should be here. And here's why we are going to be here: So that we can be a blessing:

A blessing to our family.

A blessing to our friends.

A blessing to our neighbours.

Yes, God has a purpose for you and me. One of my favourite scriptures is Ephesians 2:10. Now 8 and 9 tell us that salvation is God's business. It's an act of His grace. It's all of Him. But Ephesians 2:10 goes and says that we are…

> God's workmanship created in Christ Jesus to do good works that He has prepared in advance for us to do.

So that means if you woke up this morning and discovered that you're not dead, that's a good thing, by the way! But if you woke up this morning and discovered you're not dead, well here's the thing… God has a reason for you to be here. God has a purpose for you today. God wants you to be a blessing. Now I'll be honest with you. There's just so much stuff going on in my head and you can tell I'm super excited.

That aside. Tell me, do you know where you are going? Are you someone who knows God's blessing? Are you someone that is excited about the fact that God has you here at this time and in this very place? Living in the very place that you live? None of it is by mistake by the way.

Tell me, are you excited by the fact that God has a purpose for you? Now I will tell you one thing. If you're not, I think you need to look deep inside, because, I can tell you, my New Year is already looking up.

My hope and prayer is that your eyes are not going to be fixed on the Covid numbers and the news every night at six o'clock No, no! Our eyes are going to be fixed on Jesus, aren't they?

> Turn your eyes upon Jesus.
>
> Look full in His wonderful face
>
> and the things of earth will go strangely dim
>
> in the light of His glory and grace[9].

God has determined your times. God has determined where you should live. God has a purpose for you. This New Year is looking up no matter what the circumstances

---

9 Quotation taken from the Hymn by Helen Howarth Lemmel – O soul are you weary and burdened

are, so Happy New Year and thank you for joining me for this ‘an cupán tae with the Rev”. God bless.

January 28th 2021

The Day of Small Things…

Well folks, how's it going? It's good to be with you again for yet another 'an cupán tae with the Rev!' You know, this has been a week of small blessings. Now let me tell you something before we continue on, you know the lines from that Irish song:

> The cock could crew in the morning,
> It crew both loud and shrill,
> and I awoke in California,
> many miles away from the Spancil hill.[10]

Well there's a rooster outside my window and he's only just finding his voice. There! Did you hear him? There he goes again…

Well if he doesn't find it, it will be more than Spancil Hill

---

10 Quotation taken from the traditional song by Michael Considine - Spancil Hill (Trad. Irish Folk Song)

where he's going to be! So I apologize for his continuous intrusion. I've decided to call him Peter. You know, because poor oul' Peter, when he denied Jesus three times, the cock had crowed twice, fulfilling the words of Jesus! But this fellow is crowing the whole time. So his name's Peter! Every time I go to do a little video, he starts up in competition. Anyway, there you go!

Well, I was just about to say that in my inbox this week, there's a little blessing sent from a friend who had made two little introductory video clips for the 'an cupán tae' videos I've been making. But not only that, then another friend went and made contact with me and said, "Hey, I've got something for you!" And they sent me my very own 'an cupán tae with the Rev' mug! Now isn't that class. It's getting very official now!

So I was thinking then, that these little blessings have just encouraged me no end! I was having a conversation via text with Sam the other day. And even with that, you know, it was just very encouraging! We had a great laugh, the two us, even though we are miles apart. You know, we need to laugh.

And so as I was thinking about this 'an cupán tae' and this is what I was thinking about: God's blessings! But that's not the word that God had placed on my heart. The word that was actually on my heart which I want to share with you is found in the book of Zechariah, 4:6-10. I believe it will be a great encouragement to you.

Now, Zechariah was an Old Testament prophet and this is God speaking to Zechariah and He says,

> This is the word of the Lord to Zerubbabel. Not by might, nor by power, but by my Spirit says the Lord. What are you Almighty Mountain? Before Zerubbabel you will become level ground. Then he will bring out the capstone to shouts of, God bless it, God bless it.

Now, Zerubbabel, to let you know, is a person who is listed in the descendants of David. He had been in captivity and was returning from captivity and his desire was to go and rebuild the temple. But we'll get more into that in a second. You see God had more to say through the prophet Zechariah:

> Then the word of the Lord came to me. The hands of Zerubbabel have laid the foundation of the temple. His hands will complete it. Then you will know that the Lord Almighty has sent me to you. Do not despise the day of small things. People will rejoice when they see the plumbline in the hand of Zerubbabel.

Do not despise the day of small things! You know, this is a time where we can, and we should celebrate the small things. We get excited and we should get excited about the small things God blesses us with.

So when I open my inbox and there are two little clips for me to go and use for my 'an cupán tae' video slot, am I going to despise that? Absolutely not. That is a blessing! When I have a friend contact me, you know, and she tells me she has a gift for me, my very first official 'an cupán tae with the Rev!' mug, am I going to despise it? Make little of it? Absolutely not! It's a blessing!

When I have a chat with a friend and we have a good laugh together, am I going to just treat that with contempt!

Noooo! Because it's a blessing! These are all, believe it or not, evidence of blessings that God has given you and me.

So when you look back over your past week, who has blessed you? What are the small things you have been blessed through? That one thing that is so small it could possibly go unnoticed? I mean, after all, who's going to be looking at a piece of string in somebody's hand?

So Zerubbabel had come back to this mountain of rubble the destroyed temple of God. Everything that was precious to the people was in ruins. And as he surveyed the scene the Lord had a word for him that the people would rejoice when they just saw a plumb line in his hand. Think about that…So what is the small thing, the small way that people have blessed you this week?

But let me give you a challenge! What is a small way that you can be a blessing to somebody else? What is it that if people see what you have in your hand it is going to give them joy, brighten their world? What is it that gives them something to be ecstatic about even though they may come to you and their life is in chaos. Even though everything they dreamed about is in disarray! Even though everything that you're about is in confusion! Please don't despise the day of small things.

Folks, my prayer, my small prayer is this: No matter where you are at right now, or whatever circumstances you may be facing, I pray that God will bless you twice as much as he is blessing me, and boy, is God blessing me?! I ask Him, in Jesus' name to do this for you. Amen? Amen!

Do not despise the day of small things like having this great big 'cupán tae' and a few quiet moments to enjoy it! Have a great week. Have a blessed time. God bless. See you again soon!

February 4th 2021

Goodbye January Blues…

Welcome, welcome, welcome…

Welcome to 'an cupán tae with the Rev!' Folks, I've got to confess to you that this week I was feeling a little bit blue. I was just a little depressed in myself. And there's a couple of reasons for that. One, the Lord and I are having a disagreement. The Lord says that children are a blessing and by looking in the mirror I've discovered I'm getting very grey! AAAAAAGGGGHHHHHH!!1

But I just want to tell you something; I hadn't one grey hair before I had kids. Seriously, not one grey hair did I have before I had children. So I think that my children are the cause of this. I am now suffering from serious hair loss since I started this home-schooling lark which is another side effect of lockdown caused by Covid 19!

Also, what was getting in on me a little bit was the bald patch! Goodness me, the old patch is getting larger at the back. And yet another thing was the grey skies. The grey skies really affect me as I wear tinted glasses to help me cope with the glare! But these grey skies caused a kind of niggling headache that wouldn't go away for a few days.

Anyway, all that aside, I was outside there feeding my few cows and cleaning them out. While I was doing this, I just got to thinking about scripture. And I was thinking about what everything looked like for us at the present moment given the circumstances we find ourselves in as Christians, as people who are trying to walk with God.

We have no fellowship as the churches remain closed. We have no contact with people, unless it's through little videos, text messages, phone calls and stuff like that. So it was all just weighing on me a little bit. And I was thinking about where Elijah went and he said to the Lord, I am the only one left. And you know what, if you read that passage of scripture, you'll find modern psychology wouldn't agree with God either. The Lord basically says to Elijah, get over yourself. Cop yourself on! And that kind of happened a little bit for me. I was out there and I was just thinking about that. And the next thing, a message came in from Laura on Facebook, which just said:

Be faithful in what the Lord has given you!

You know, it's a bit like one of those kick up the backside moments! So I said, "Okay, Lord!" For me it was the same as the Lord meeting up with Elijah and saying, "Get over yourself!".

As you know, there are four thousand other people who haven't served Baal. You're not the only one. Cop yourself on there! So I have to say that that really helped me to kind of cop on myself. But this week the great skies were really getting to me. Then I noticed the Psalm that is assigned for this week, for this Sunday. Listen to what it says here in Psalm 147:7-9:

> Sing to the Lord with thanksgiving. Make music to our God on the harp. He covers the sky with clouds. He supplies the earth with rain and makes grass grow on the hills. He provides food for the cattle and for the young ravens when they call.

I thought, what a verse! I'll have to read it again! He covers the sky with clouds. He supplies the earth with rain and makes grass grow on hills. He provides food for the cattle and for the young ravens when they call.

Do you know, here we are in this country and we're always moaning about the rain. Oh, it's raining again. Now, in fairness, we've had a lot of rain. And some of my fields are underwater. I'm just like: Oh no, it's raining again. Oh, my goodness, oh, it's just terrible. And I'm there going, oh, the skies are grey. Oh, it's wrecking my head! Aaaaaah!

But here, the Psalmist says: Sing to the Lord. Why? Because God has covered the sky with clouds. So when you get up and you look out and you see a cloudy day, you have to thank God. When you look at the fact that the Lord provides for the animals in the field, for the cattle, that means that if they're getting grass and fed and everything else, then you're getting your milk, cheese, butter, yogurt, meat, everything on the shelf. So the Lord is providing for you by providing for them.

And I love that verse about the ravens. Now, the closest thing we have to the raven in this country is the crow. And all the crows for some reason decide to sit on the telephone wire, just outside our house. Every evening they all gather! Well, morning and evening, they all gather up there. I'm not joking! But it goes and says, 'when they call' so that means they actually go and call to the Lord and He provides them with food. Well, I tell you one thing, it's like a chaotic sort of prayer meeting outside every night in my place with them. They are all calling and praying to God at the same time. Every one of them, CAW, CAW, CAW, CAW, CAW. Now, I mean no disrespect, but do you know what? Those crows really have God's ear!

So every time you see a whole pile of crows… Crows of all things! Remember, God's blessing you! Isn't that amazing? But here's the thing… when we see clouds: we are blessed…when we see the green grass growing: we are blessed. When we see the rain: we are blessed. When we go and see the crows, creating an awful racket on a wire: it's a sign that we are blessed!

Do you know what? Living in this country, folks, we are blessed. Even though the skies might be grey. Even though the crows are annoying. Even though Peter is crowing outside, it all reminds us that we are in a place of blessing! Yes, we are in a place of blessing!

So do you feel blessed? Well it's time to say goodbye to those January blues. Time to say goodbye to those springtime blues. It's time for us to sing to the Lord with thanksgiving and to make music to him on the harp. You know, maybe, like me, you were having a bit of a blue week. And what you needed from the Lord was just such a word: "Get over it!"

Sure it's not nice to hear sometimes, but sometimes that's exactly what we need to hear. Like that little text from Laura, which just went and said: 'Be faithful to what the Lord has given you.' Tell me how are you being faithful today? Are you singing even though the skies are grey? Or, when you see the crows on the wire? Or, when you see green grass growing? Or, when you see the rain falling? If not, maybe it's time for you to change and kick them blues into touch!

February 11th 2021

Love, Work and St. Valentine

Welcome to 'an cupán tae with the Rev' and a very good morning to you. I have to tell you Valentine's Day is coming. I have my Valentine's love heart tie on. I have my piece of paper here to do some writing to get ready to think about what romantic message I'm going to send. But I decided to actually check up on who St. Valentine is. And do you know what's very interesting about St. Valentine? They actually know nothing about him. And in regard to love and cards and all that sort of stuff, there's nothing. Well, actually a hundred years after he had died they said:

> Here is a man who is revered by men
> and whose works are best known by God.

What's that got to do with Valentine's Day? Or love? Or anything else for that matter? Anyway, the thing is he died on February 14th. He was actually martyred by Claudius II for his faith. I think that's very interesting. Do you not think that is very interesting? And here we are, sending cards, you know, declaring our undying love to our boyfriends or girlfriends or to secret admirers, to husbands, wives and all the rest of it. So anyway, I was just thinking, seeing that St Valentine was martyred, I would write maybe…

Roses are red,
Violets are blue,
St Valentine's a martyr,
and so are you!

What do you think about that one? Or here is a different one…

Roses are red,
Violets are blue,
Saint Valentine's dead,
and so are you!

I don't know if that would really work - sounds a little bit violent! Anyway, forget that nonsense, the thing is that when it comes to romance my Grandmother said to me one day: 'Why all this fuss about one day in the year? If my husband doesn't romantically love me for 365 days, we can forget it

if he's only going to show up on one!'

I thought that was fantastic. I liked that. So I've decided I don't turn up for any at all. No point in putting on a special effort for one day. Just be who you are. But here's the thing, I got thinking about it, you know, when we were going out together, Queen Victoria and me. We ended up having to go along to a marriage counselling course before we got married, preparation for marriage, that kind of thing, I don't know what to call it. And one of the key points of advice that we were given was that the best things in life require work and so does marriage. Well, I don't know about his marriage, but I tell you one thing, my marriage is brilliant. Being married to Queen Victoria is just a win-win situation and I'm the one who's doing all the winning!

Now, please don't ask her because you might get a different story. But I am doing all the winning, no doubt about it. So folks, if it's not broke, why fix it? Do you know what I mean?

But I tell you, this got me really thinking about a scripture today as a result of discovering that St Valentine was martyred for his faith. Claudius II, we are led to believe, actually really liked St Valentine, but the thing that really upset him was that St Valentine kept telling him that he needed to repent, that he needed to accept Christ as his Saviour. Now as Emperor of Rome, Claudius II wasn't very happy about that and so he decided to martyr him, get rid of him, kill him off. Well, he didn't say I will martyr him. He did say he was going to get rid of him. And so St. Valentine was martyred for his faith.

I've been working my way through John's gospel and a verse of scripture, talking about work and the best things in life requiring work I found is John 6:29. And this is one of those moments where a lot of people actually deserted Jesus. They gave up on Jesus. And that got me thinking about where we are at and with all that's going on. Now, be assured I'm not giving up on Jesus. Don't worry about that. But the thing that really struck me is what it says:

> The work of God is this, to believe in the one He has sent.

Those are Jesus' words, that the work of God is this, to believe in the one He has sent. But when we consider St Valentine, he actually declared his undying love for Jesus

Christ right up to the point where he died. Claudius II asked him to renounce his faith to give up on God, to quit. But he wouldn't do it. Well, maybe that's where we get the whole thing about showing our undying love.

But that also reminds us that God has shown His undying love for us through the death of Jesus Christ. That's why it says in Romans 5.8:

> But God demonstrated his love for us in that while we were yet sinners, Christ died for us.

Right, but to this Valentine's day poem. Hmmm… Roses are red. Violets are blue… Oh I've got it. I've got it.

Roses are red.
Violets are blue.
This an cupán tae's
Specially for you!

Happy St. Valentine's day and I pray that you know that GOD LOVES YOU!

February 18th 2021

A Garment of Praise!

Welcome to 'an cupán tae with the Rev!' I have to tell you folks, I'm really excited. And the thing that is exciting me is this. I'm back looking at Isaiah 61 again which is about the year of the Lord's Favour. I'll just read it to you and then I will explain why I'm excited. Part of the Lord's favour is what Isaiah was charged by the Lord to declare at the time. This was what Isaiah was to do…

He was to proclaim the year of the Lord's favour and the day of the vengeance of our God. Why? "To comfort all who mourn."

So what he was going to say was going to comfort all who mourn and provide for those who grieve in Zion. But it doesn't stop there as it states in Isaiah 61:3b that he was:

> To bestow on them a crown of beauty instead of ashes. To bestow on them the oil of gladness instead of mourning. To bestow on them a garment of praise instead of a spirit of despair.

And I have to tell you, the garment of praise thing has really been buzzing in my mind. I'll get into that a little bit more, but here's the thing: A garment is an item of clothing. Now if I am cold I would stick on my body warmer. And, Hey Presto! it keeps me warm. So I am putting on a garment. So I have now put on my garment which is keeping me warm, it has impacted my circumstances. So too in the same way the garment of praise impacts the circumstances of one in despair!

Now 'to bestow' something upon someone means to 'give a gift of something to someone. So the Lord is exhorting Isaiah to give a gift of the garment of praise to the one in despair!

Praise is not something that comes naturally to us, it is something we have to put on. Put on the garment of praise instead of a spirit of despair! You have to put on a garment of praise.

So here we are. We have been given this garment. Put it on! I would have to say for me, praise is not something that comes naturally. You know, I'm not someone who is there going, Whoo hooooo!

There are people who are like that. and I think that is

amazing. They are just so in awe, praising the Lord for this, that and the other thing! Praising the Lord for everything around them. They see the goodness of the Lord in everything!

Well, I am not one of those people. I am a bit more reserved, withdrawn, more of a questioning type of person. And so, you know, you stick on the garment of praise. It's something that doesn't come naturally. So it's something that sometimes we have to go and put on.

Now, what really strikes me is that it's exciting, and that's what I am telling you about. This is exciting… Paul, in 2 Corinthians 1:3-4 says:

> Praise be to the God and Father of our Lord Jesus Christ, the Father of compassion and the God of all comfort who comforts us in all our troubles.

Isn't that brilliant? The God of all comfort comforts us in all our troubles so that we can comfort those in any trouble with the comfort we ourselves have received from God!... Man! That blows my mind!

Now here's the thing, he's saying, look, we need to praise God for this. Praise God. The God and Father of our Lord Jesus Christ. Why? Because he is a father of compassion and he comforts us during our troubles. So now let me ask you: what is it that's troubling you? What is it that's upsetting you?

There's a chorus that goes:

> Praise him praise him,
> praise him in the morning,
> praise him in the noon time,
> praise him, praise him,
> praise him the whole day through.[11]

But the thing is, very often we can come to a point where we're wondering: what is there to praise God for?

Well, if you have a Bible and look into it, you will find that people praise God for everything. They praise God for his provision. They praise God for their food. One

---

[11] Author unknown

lady went and praised God that she had four sons! Some simply praised God for the fact that God had blessed them. In fact, other people went to praise God because somebody else was blessed.

But today, do you need a garment of praise to be given to you? To be bestowed upon you? Maybe it's just to lift you at this present moment in your troubles and to realize that God is who He says He is: The God of comfort, the God of compassion.

But as you experience God blessing you and comforting you, turn around and comfort your neighbour or your friend. You know, that's a thing that's really been striking me a lot lately about Christianity. Christianity is all about God blessing me, but not only that. All my blessing can be a blessing to those around me! And then when I find that my life isn't that, that I'm not being blessed, well how could my life bless anybody?

The whole point is that I've to realize that it is all about God… It is God who is the one who is blessing me! It is God who is the God of compassion, the God of comfort. And that God is comforting me in my troubles. So it's not saying that we're trouble free, but God is blessing me in my troubles so that I can go and bless you in your troubles.

So how can I help you to put on that garment of praise? Let me just say this, whatever you're going through today, please put on the garment of praise. Don't be overcome by a spirit of despair!

Praise him in the morning. Praise him in the noon time. Praise him the whole day through. Why? Because the God of compassion is comforting you today. What a blessing! You may not see it, but what a blessing!

February 25th 2021

Another Gift and Chainsaw Oil

Welcome to our 'an cupán tae with the Rev.' As you can see I'm outside today and I'm doing a little bit of maintenance on my chainsaw. Josh and I woke up one day last week and we decided to be lumberjacks for a day or two. In this part of the country you would call a lumberjack a tree surgeon nowadays. Anyway, we were just chopping up some firewood from a tree that had fallen down.

So, in servicing my chainsaw, I have to go and use some two stroke fuel so I can get the chainsaw going again. Some chainsaw oil and some oil of joy, just to keep everything going. Ha ha! I had you going there! Now you are wondering why I am using the oil of joy for it?

Well actually the oil of joy is the very thing that I've been thinking about these past few days. Again I'm back in Isaiah 61 and I have to say this passage of scripture has really got me super-excited. The oil of joy, it says in Isaiah, is another one of the gifts that God has asked us to bestow on one another.

Another one of the things that we can bless one another with is this, the year of the Lord's favour as I've said. People, this is the year of the Lord's favour, make no mistake about it, and so the oil of joy is one of those blessings listed in this passage of scripture. Listen to what it says here in Isaiah 61:2-3…

> To proclaim the year of the Lord's favour and the day of the vengeance of our God, to comfort all who mourn, and provide for those who grieve in Zion - to bestow on them a crown of beauty instead of ashes, the oil of joy instead of mourning, and a garment of praise instead of a spirit of despair. They will be called oaks of righteousness, a planting of the Lord for the display of his splendour.

Now very often when we think about mourning, we only think about it in the context of death, of someone dying, but it's not necessarily just about that. It could also be to do with the death of the way of life as we know it and these people in Isaiah's time, well they were in places where they'd been removed from home. It ended up that they were displaced. They had lost their income. They'd lost their work. They'd lost their homes. They'd gone through a terrible time and we can identify with some of that as some of us are under the cosh right now. We're finding it tough going and so we could be actually mourning for the life that we once had.

The other thing is that we could be mourning the lack of normality, just being with our friends. Being able to meet up for a coffee. A friend and I were having a conversation on Zoom the other day and we were saying 'here's to the day that we're going to actually end up having a coffee face to face again' It's almost like the way the people of Israel, the Jews used to always say after celebrating the Passover, 'Next year in Jerusalem!' So here we are, saying something similar, 'Here's to the time that we're going to be able to sit down and have fun together.'

But at this present moment in time we are mourning that reality. Mourning that norm. Mourning the reality of not being able to have fellowship in person with our brothers and sisters where God is with us. Mourning that intimacy.

And yet, God is with us all right now. He is here in our mourning; God offers us His gift of the oil of joy. Do you not need the gift of the oil of joy? I know that the topic of joy is something that just fascinates me. It's something that I just really love to dig into, to understand. To be honest with you, the more that I try to look into it the less I seem to understand it, because it's just so phenomenal.

Now, see this is the thing; real joy is mine no matter what circumstances I find myself in, and it is the same for you. It is all about knowing the joy of God in the midst of whatever hardship you find yourself in! But added to this, with the oil of joy, an anointing has been placed upon a person. This happened for someone who was going to be anointed king. Now when Jesus Christ quotes this passage in Luke, He states that God had anointed Him. So when we think of Jesus Christ, at this time of Lent, we think of Him being the suffering person, we think of Him being the person who died on the cross. Very often that is continuously a picture of Jesus Christ that we are presented with but He's actually someone who blesses us with the oil of joy.

After all, the joy of the Lord is our strength and so today maybe what you and I need is that fresh anointing of the oil of joy in our lives so that we can see things beyond where we're at in this present moment. Now my prayer for you, my prayer for me, is that we would bestow upon one another the oil of joy, no matter if the teardrops start, because we've found the secret - Jesus in our hearts. You know no matter what the storm, no matter what we're going through, when Christ is with us we have nothing to fear because our lives are hidden with Christ in God. That thought alone, just in itself, is some oil of joy.

So just as I needed some oil to lubricate the chain of my chainsaw, just as I needed the oil to mix into the petrol so my chainsaw is going to run, so too we need the oil of joy in our lives. With it we know we can live on an even keel, knowing the blessing and the wonder and the majesty of God in our lives. Let's not lose focus on who God is for us even in these days.

Now I've got to go and chop some timber so until next time the Lord bless you all. Thank you for joining me for this 'cupán tae,' Talk to you again soon and God bless.

March 4th 2021

Trading Ashes!

Welcome to 'an cupán tae with the Rev!' I'm here to do a business deal so I hope you have the oul' kettle on, as we get down to business! One of the things that I really enjoy is looking at pawn show programmes on TV. You see people bringing in some weird and wonderful stuff. Then there's a whole explanation of what that weird and wonderful stuff is. Then after that the haggling begins between the potential seller and the pawnbroker. The seller names their asking price and sometimes they sell it for more, sometimes they sell it for less or they don't sell it at all! I enjoy the whole process of all this excitement taking place.

When I was a bass guitarist in a worship band many years ago, it ended up that there was a song out at the time and this was a firm favourite of the people. The lyrics really were on my mind today and really got me thinking. The song was all about wheeling and dealing and trading this, that and the other thing.

And everyone loved it because of the chorus and they would all be jumping around, waving their arms in the air, singing at the tops of their voices.

Anyway, I used to be thumping it out on the bass back in the day, but the memory of that really got me thinking, about what we've been looking at over the last few weeks in Isaiah 61. I'm thinking: "Hang on a second! So this is a bit like heading to a pawn broker's where we're walking in and we're having a conversation with God trying to hammer out a business deal!

So I've decided I want to do a business deal today because the verse I'm looking at in Isaiah 61 is all about ashes. So imagine you're walking into the store and you put this big bag of ashes on the counter and then God comes over to you and goes, 'So what's this?' And you reply, 'Well, it's a big bag…of ashes, they are very special ashes, they are my ashes, but well… the thing is that I would like to trade these ashes in for the Joy of the Lord. I think it's a fair deal, don't you?'

Can you imagine how God feels when we come up with that sort of stuff? Now I understand that in the context of the song they're talking about swapping these things for the joy of the Lord, but even so it's still not right! And here when we look at Isaiah 61:3, what does it say? It says:

> To bestow on them a crown of beauty
> instead of ashes,
> the oil of joy instead of mourning,
> and a garment of praise instead of a spirit
> of despair.
> They will be called oaks of righteousness,
> a planting of the Lord for the display of his
> splendour.

You see the thing is that the Lord is bestowing it upon us! It's a gift! He's placing a gift on you! He's placing a gift on me! And this verse goes and says: to bestow on them a crown of beauty instead of ashes!

So God isn't going, "I'll tell you what, let's do business here. No, no, I'm not going to give you the joy of the Lord for your ashes. I am going to give you a crown of beauty. God isn't saying, "Let's do a deal, let's see, so now you have one large bag of ashes, well that means that you get one large crown of beauty doesn't it…"

No, God has bestowed upon you… God has given you… It is instead of… It's not that he's going to say: "Let's trade, let's swap this". God is actually saying: "I'm giving you this gift. Get rid of the ashes, get rid of them! I'm giving you a gift, I am bestowing this upon you, I'm presenting you with this crown of beauty".

And you know, when I was thinking about it, it reminds me of the prodigal son and the reality is that we're all in that position, even the older brother in that story is a prodigal son because he has missed the joy of being at the party. He has missed the fun of being with the father. 'All these years I've been working with you and you haven't even given me a goat for a party.' And the father turns around and says, 'But son, it's all yours, you can have a party anytime!'

But the point is, when we look at this, the prodigal son is there covered in muck, sitting in the middle of the field with pigs all around him and he's looking at the food that the pigs are eating and he's thinking: Oh I wish I could eat that food, I'm so hungry! But he doesn't go and say, 'Do you know what I'll do? I'll go home and do a business deal!

But he doesn't. because the focus would then be on him… I will do this, I will do that…, You know, I will do a deal and I will trade in these old pig smelling clothes for this or that…!

No, no, no, no, no, no, this is all about God! God is the one who has given us His gift, the gift of a crown of beauty. God is the one who has given us the gift of a garment of praise. God is the one who has given us the gift of the oil of joy. God has bestowed these things upon us.

And so when the prodigal son comes back with it all worked out in his head and he goes to deliver his little rehearsed speech: 'Father you know I have sinned against you and against God and I've sinned against everyone and… and please, all I'm asking is that you just make me a servant'… The father says, 'No way! You are my son!' And the father goes and calls his servants and says: 'Come on, come on, come on, quick, let's throw a party here. Find a fresh robe, put a ring on his finger, let's go and get him washed and cleaned up, and let's do this, let's do that'…

And it's all about the extravagance of the father! And so what excites me while we are having this little 'an cupán tae' is when I think about that! The extravagance of God!

It's not about trading. God isn't interested in doing a trade. We could never pay for what He has on offer. In fact, it isn't about trading anything. It is all about accepting the beautiful gifts that God has given us. And God has given us the gift of a crown of beauty instead of the ashes! God has given us the gift of a garment of praise instead of the spirit of despair. God has given us a gift of the oil of joy instead of mourning, and so my life is running on that beautiful and even keel. I'm anointed, I am blessed, I am crowned. Now, I don't know about you, but I can't help but be excited!

So, guess what? I think I'm just going to bring my bag of ashes to the dump, and I'm just going to enjoy the wonderful gifts that God has given me! Today, don't lose focus on the gifts that God has blessed you with. Till next time, enjoy this old 'cupán tae!' God bless!

March 11th 2021

Mother's Day, Comfort, Ma and God

Welcome to 'an cupán tae with the Rev.' Well, folks, guess what? Today I'm designing a little picture for Mother's Day. As you know, Sunday is coming and it's Happy Mother's Day and so I have drawn my self-portrait as a little hedgehog, prickly and sensitive creature that I am! I am drawing a flower, the sun shining, and everything's perfect. A lovely scene!

So Happy Mother's Day. You see, my mother and I, we're really quite close. I would just like to let you all know that. Yes, we are really quite close as she only lives 11 miles away! All joking aside we are very close. See, the reason that we're very close is I'm the one who has bestowed upon her the title of "Mother". And so even though my siblings came afterwards, it was I who gave her that name. It was I who went and had the title bestowed upon her for the rest of her life up to this point as "Ma". Just like when Joshua, our eldest lad, was born. He was the one who bestowed upon my mother the title of "Granny." So I mean, both of us are very privileged people, Joshua and I, that we were able to bestow upon my mother these wonderful names.

But don't be getting upset, You see I'm also very close to my mother-in-law because she lives the same distance away but in a different direction! Anyway, now that I have cleared that up, I was looking at and researching the whole idea about Mother and looking up Christian songs and things about Mother and you know what? I discovered they are very morose and depressing. Every one of the songs is written from the viewpoint that Mother is dead. So I thought that wasn't really a great idea for Mother's Day.

Anyway, Queen Victoria and I went shopping the other day and when we were in the shop, she asked me: "Are you going to buy a Happy Mother's Day card for your mother?" I was like, "What? Buy my mother a card? Do you want me to give my mother a heart attack? She would think I went and bumped my head or I'm in need of psychiatric care or something. That would be completely out of the blue."

And then I started to read some of the things inside the cards. As I sat there reading, I thought, I can't sign this because the first thing my mother's going to say to me is, "Son, didn't I tell you? Don't tell lies."

> Mother, you are one in a million, you're the best thing since sliced pan. You're the greatest person I've ever known. You're always there. You're so wonderful. You're so brilliant.

My mother is all those things. But when it is all written in a card like that it is just so corny, it's just like, "bleeeeh", so cringe-worthy, please pass me a bucket sort of stuff! But, back to the songs whether it's "Will the circle be unbroken", where your man's thinking about how he is going to be one day reunited with his mother who died as they're travelling along behind the hearse! Or there are songs where the writer is reflecting on his or her Mother's prayers and life of faith after she has gone and they themselves have come on hard times. Real heartwarming stuff for all mothers to look forward to indeed. I mean, "Really?" I enjoy the conversations I have with my mother now while she's alive, never mind, pondering on them when she is dead. That's ridiculous stuff.

Anyway, the other thing that just really struck me with all this is Jesus. When his mother and brothers came along, you know, He was inside the house having a conversation, talking to people and the place was packed. Some of the folk there said to Jesus, 'just to let you know, your mother and brothers are outside.' In Matthew 12:50 we read Jesus' response:

> "Who is my mother? Who are my brothers?" Pointing to his disciples, He said, "Here are my mother and my brothers. For whoever does the will of my Father in heaven is my brother and sister and mother."

I think that seems a bit disingenuous as well, at least to my way of thinking. Even though the point He's making is that those of us who follow Him are like a mother and brother to him. But I love this verse in Isaiah 66:13. I think this is beautiful. God states:

> As a mother comforts her child, so I will comfort you. You shall be comforted in Jerusalem.

Very often, God is portrayed as being this patriarchal figure, always as father, but here is an exception. Now, as I have said, the context of this is that the people were displaced and are now living in Babylon. They've been taken from their homes. They've been deprived of everything. And what the Lord is saying is, 'I'm going to put all things back and the place that I'm going to comfort you in is your own home.' It's amongst your own people in that sense of belonging. but it's not only that, the Lord goes and says, 'I will be like a mother to you and I will comfort you.' Isn't that beautiful?

Now everyone of us here had a mother or still does have a mother. And so as we ponder this verse, God has given us something very simple, a little picture of who He is. How many times, as a small child, did you end up falling and your mother was there and picked you up? Or when you ended up grazing your knee, your mother was the one who put a bandage on it? Or when you were having a tough time in school and your mother was the person who listened to you? Or you ended up facing difficult decisions, such as choosing school or college, or what career you might like, and it was your mother who was there for you as that sounding block of reason. And God in this passage is saying, that's who I am. Whatever you're going through right now, whatever your problems are, whatever your hassles are, whatever is destroying your world, whatever is getting to you, I am like a mother looking after her child. I am going to comfort you.

But with a mother that doesn't stop, does it? Nor does it with God. Now just take a moment and ponder on the love of God as we are coming towards Mother's Day and all those cards and all that other stuff that goes with it. When you look at your mother or think about your mother, may it bring back an image of who God is and how God loves and cares and comforts you. Send those cards folks, but don't be telling your mother any lies. Have a happy Mother's Day and remember, that's how God comforts you! Amen.

March 18th 2021

Light that Fire…

Good morning and welcome to 'an cupán tae with the Rev'. Anyway, I know what you're all thinking, you're going: "Hey, do you not know that St. Patrick's Day was soooooo yesterday!" Well, do you know what? A good party is one that carries on and so you could say that this is the morning after the night before! Now, I just want to say firstly a big thank you to all who joined us for the seisiún last night. 120 people turned up to the cabin via YouTube and you can still check that out. The video is up on YouTube but a big thank you to all who joined us for our little seisiún last night.

Now, one of the things that intrigues me, that excites me when I think about St. Patrick is all the fantastic stories that go around. Some of them are legends, myths and then there are some things that are real. And one of the things that is real, which is the story that we all know as we've all heard it, is about the day that he went and lit a fire on the mountain.

Now, it was the custom of the time that all the lights and fires would be put out. Then the high king would go and light a fire and then all the fires would be lit all around. And so you'd see this beacon of hope shining through the community. But the key component was the high king had to light the fire first. And of course St. Patrick went and stole a march on the king, he pulled a quick one and went ahead and lit the fire first on the Hill of Tara. Naturally, of course, that caused trouble, actually uproar! And so the people had to find out why it was that St. Patrick went and lit his fire first. How dare he go and light it before the high king!

Well, as you know, then St. Patrick went and shared about Jesus Christ being the light of the world. But I would like us to think of this from a different angle, and so I'm back in Isaiah chapter 61 and as I've said to you before, this is the year of the Lord's favour. When we look at St. Patrick and we consider the fire that he lit and the fact that he spoke of Jesus as the light of the world, what was he doing? Well, Isaiah 61:1-2a states:

> The Spirit of the Sovereign Lord is on me, because the Lord has anointed me to proclaim good news to the poor. He has sent me to bind up the brokenhearted, to proclaim freedom for the captives and release from darkness for the prisoners, to proclaim the year of the Lord's favour.

So as a part of the year of the Lord's favour, the good news would be proclaimed and that good news is that Jesus Christ is the light of the world. And here's why it's good news. It tells us that in the year of the Lord's favour there will be a release from darkness for the prisoners.

Now how many of us, even in our society today, are caught up in darkness? Darkness of the mind, darkness of psychology, (you want to say, hey, the same thing). Darkness of spirits, even the mood around us can just bring us down. And so today we have reason to celebrate, just as they had back then. The fact that St. Patrick came and brought that good news to our land and told us - this is exciting! But here's the thing I also want to bring out to you: "You are the light of the world.' I'm quoting Jesus in Matthew 5:14!

You are someone who brings hope. You are someone who brings joy. You are someone who can bless others. And if you are someone who professes to be a Christian, irrespective of what tradition or denomination you come from, that's who you are! You are the light of the world. Now when you look in the mirror, is that what you think?

Do you think: I am someone who is bringing light to this world. I am someone who is making this world a better place. I am someone who brings joy to this world. I am someone who brings happiness. I am someone who brings blessing to everybody I meet.

Sadly, the thing is that most of us don't have that sort of mentality. We don't actually go and think that we are someone who brings light to the world. Some of us, like St. Patrick, have to go and climb the hill first. We have to go and climb up that mountain before we can light that fire. But what I want to say to you today is, you are the light of the world. And here's why… Jesus Christ said so! And if

you hear any other little voice in your head, any other little thing saying in your head: 'No, that's not me. I have nothing to contribute. I can't bring any light to anyone.

I am someone who is just… or, if you had a life like mine,

Nigel, you wouldn't even talk like this. Nigel if you understood my circumstances…'

But that's not what Jesus said. Jesus said that you are the light of the world. It's a fact. It's a statement. So today, the day after Saint Patrick's day, I want to ask you a question: Are you going to light that fire? Are you going to walk in the belief of who Jesus Christ said you are? Are you going to light up your world? Bring joy, peace, blessing… because you are that very person!

So let us go. Let us light our fire on the top of our hill of Tara and let us be, as Jesus said, the light of the world. because that's who He said we are. So let us be who we are!

April 1st 2021

Confessions and Contemplations…

Welcome to 'an cupán tae 'with the Rev,' and folks, today is Holy Thursday and I am pondering Easter, Resurrection Day, and why Jesus had to die. So yeah, it is heavy stuff! I was listening to the radio some time back when a commentator was talking to the presenter about law-breaking.

He gave the example of people driving on the motorway. Even though the speed limit is 120 kilometres per hour and he was doing the limit, he found that many people were breaking the law. Now just because it was a community where everybody does it, that doesn't mean that it's right! I got thinking about that and here's my confession…

I remembered a time when I was driving up and down the motorway which I had to do a lot, especially when I was going to Belfast. I would set the cruise control on the car to 125 kilometres per hour even though the limit is 120 kilometres! Now, that's only 5 kilometres over the limit, so I mean, come on, how big of a deal is that!? Sure it's only 5 kilometres after all! But, the thing is that if a squad car was to come, blue lights flashing, that could be a whole different story!

Now another confession is I don't like to hear, nor do I like to see blue lights on the motorway. One of the reasons is simply that it's the Guards,[12] and the second is it normally means that there is an accident further up the road. The thing is, it always brought a negative feeling over me when I saw blue lights.

But the other thing is that the Garda car represents the law. So even though you might be doing 5 kilometres over or 100 kilometres over, as soon as you see that Garda car, it brings conviction of sin. And you see that's the whole point. But the question nowadays is: what is sin? People are asking me that question. So what is sin?

Sin is to transgress the law. It's to break the law. And a very simple example of what it means to sin, at least in regard to road usage, is when you drive faster than you should. And then what reinforces your understanding of

---

[12] "The Guards" is a colloquialism meaning the Irish Garda (Police force)

your sin is when you see the law in the form of a Garda car, blue lights flashing, coming up behind you!

Now, when it comes to Jesus Christ and His sacrifice, and what that is all about and why, we've been looking at what Jesus does for us. We've been looking at the blessings that Jesus brings. We've been looking at joy. We've been looking at the wonders of, and the greatness of what God has done for us. And God has done wonderful things for us all through the person of Jesus Christ.

Here is why: Jesus is the person who has saved us from the punishment of the law. So let's continue our example and we'll get to the sacrifice of Jesus in a second. Imagine you end up… now in my case, thank God this didn't happen, although I did get points on my licence once, but let's imagine you get pulled in by the guards for speeding. And the guard issues the fine.

Now it's come to a point where, not only are you guilty of transgressing the law, but secondly the law has come down on top of you with force and has issued the fine. So you are now in a position of condemnation under the law, and that could mean a speeding fine of three points on your licence or worse!

And in the same way, God's ten commandments, which we hear very little about nowadays come into operation. But if you want to ignore the four commandments about God, although I think they're very, very important, the other six are about how your neighbours would like you to treat them, and also how you would like your neighbours to treat you.

After all you don't want your neighbour to run off with your wife or your husband. You don't want your neighbour to steal your goods. You don't want your neighbour to kill you. You don't want your neighbour to dishonour you, to be a false witness against you. So the thing is this, the very fact you don't want your neighbour to do these things to you, should make you think about not doing those things to your neighbour?

That is what the law reveals, and yet we all find ourselves in a place where we are condemned by that law. An example of this is where Jesus says if you go and look lustfully at someone, you've broken the law, you've committed adultery in your heart.

So why did Jesus come to die? Jesus came to die to save us because we stand condemned already under the law. So if you go back to our story, imagine someone came along and you were going to lose your licence. You're going to be put off the road. You're never going to be able to drive again.

And then someone came and said, 'I'll take that. I'll take that blame. You can take my licence. You can put me off the road.' Ultimately, that's what Jesus Christ did. Jesus said: 'No, I'll be the one who takes the punishment.' Scripture in Romans 3:20 states:

> Therefore, no one will be declared righteous in God's sight by observing the law. Rather, through the law, we become conscious of our sin.

When you're driving on the motorway at 125 km or more, and you see those blue lights flashing, you become conscious of your sin, and you are reminded of the death of Jesus and what he suffered. Be conscious of the fact that you need him as a Saviour! After all, none of us has kept the law, God's law that is!

Serious thoughts, serious confessions. I leave it with you. Thanks for joining me for this 'cupán tae,' and a Happy Resurrection Day by the way.

April 15th 2021

Shortcuts, Freedom and a 'Licence' to Ignore the Law… Really?

Way Heeeeeeeyyyy and welcome back to "an cupán tae with the Rev!' and yeah I'm back from a week's holiday and as you can hear Peter is still crowing away outside there. Well, I just wanted to talk to you about a trip that I made to India. Back in the day the Unchained Gang MM Irish chapter had a bike run called the Hope Run for the children in an orphanage in India. So when I went to India on other business I decided to visit the orphanage.

But I want to share a story about the time I was with my friend Ratnaraj and we were riding around India on our motorbikes and it ended up that we went and…

Well I'll just read you a story from Matthew 5:17-20 first! I'm reading it to you so that you can understand the story I'm going to tell you regarding the law. So, Jesus says:

> "Do you think that I have come to abolish the law or the prophets? I have not come to abolish them but to fulfill them. I tell you the truth, until heaven and earth disappear not the smallest letter nor the least stroke of a pen will by any means disappear from the law until everything is accomplished. Therefore, anyone who breaks one of the least of these commandments and teaches others to do the same will be called the least in the kingdom of heaven, but whoever practises and teaches the commands will be called great in the kingdom of heaven. For I tell you that unless your righteousness surpasses that of the Pharisees and the teachers of the law you will certainly not enter the kingdom of heaven."

So, what the Lord is actually saying is that we are supposed to be people who are living not under the law but as a fulfillment of the law. Our lives should be an example of that and we shouldn't be leading others astray!

Well now let me tell you a little story. As I've said, Ratnaraj, my good friend and I were going around India on our motorbikes and talking about leading people astray!

We were riding along a motorway and the next thing, we crossed the motorway into the fast lane. Now there was nothing thankfully coming and we slowed down to practically a full stop in the fast lane as there was a section of curbs taken up out of the centre island of the motorway which we went through to the opposite side of the motorway travelling into the oncoming traffic!!!

Now I hasten to tell you I am the tourist here and I didn't know where I was going, so I was following Ratnaraj! Also I can't go and say it was the blind leading the blind as I was the only one who was really blind to what was going on here. I hadn't a clue where we were going other than that we were most definitely going down the wrong side of the motorway heading towards the oncoming traffic. This was thankfully spasmodic. Then we cut across the two lanes of traffic to the hard shoulder on the far side where we came to a slip road down to a roundabout!

But the problem was, we went down the slip road used by the traffic to join the motorway! So now we were entering the roundabout from the wrong side Rather than going around the roundabout as you should, Oh no! no! we went and cut across a roundabout, onto one of the feeder roads - again on the wrong side, as it was the road heading for home!

This, I was informed afterwards, was a shortcut! Now consider the number of traffic violations that the two of us had committed on that little trip! Apart from the near death experience we were committed to, just think about it. Here is a classic example of someone, my friend in this case, leading someone astray!

Now I will admit, I was easily led astray because I hadn't a clue where I was going or how to get to our destination. Also, I don't know what we actually achieved by doing this, considering we could have just gone straight down the motorway on our own side, come to the slip road going down to the roundabout on our own side, under the flyover and out to where we had come, all legally, safely and with no threat to anyone's life!

So needless to say, Ratnaraj and I had a big conversation about all this! It was, believe it or not, only one of many interesting biking experiences I had in India!

Now when I think of the law and think of God, which is one of the things I've been doing this past while, especially being focused on Jesus Christ dying on the cross and thinking about the law in that context, it occurred to me that very often as Christians we think when Jesus died on the cross that we've been saved from under the law. We claim that the law means nothing to us anymore, believing we have freedom to do whatever we want. After all Paul tells us in Galatians 5:1:

> "It is for freedom that Christ has set us free!"

Absolutely it is! But that does not mean we are now called to be lawless. No! It means we are supposed to be people who are living within the law, law abiding, who live according to the law. We are supposed to be a righteous people! A people who are in an upright place. especially in regard to God's law. So one of the little things I've been doing as an experiment of late: I've just been asking people and I'm also going to ask you this question as we're having our cup of tea. How many of the ten commandments do you know?

An interesting question. You know I have been discovering that very few people seem to know any of the ten commandments, or even a few of the ten for that matter.

So if we don't know the law then we're living according to our own rules and regulations, so we're living in a lawless society. Lately a friend of mine lost her husband and she very kindly invited me to the funeral via YouTube seeing as the numbers who can attend due to Covid are smaller, and I was really blessed by it.

One of the things that I liked was the 'drive-through' around the GAA club which he had been very involved in. When the funeral cortege drove into the yard and came to a stop, the main guys of the club who were there just shared their thoughts, and they went on to talk about how this person was now before the 'Great Referee' - meaning God, and it occurred to me that the referee is someone who is responsible for upholding the law! Jesus in this passage goes and says:

> I'm not removing any of the law! Know this, there's not one bit going to be taken away even though I am the fulfillment of the law!

How often though do we actually treat God like a referee? Look at any football or hurling match, the poor referee gets some doing! The referee's always getting roasted by the players and the spectators! There's always that sense of injustice. How dare he blow the whistle! How dare he call a foul! How dare he do this! How dare he do that!

Let's be honest! that is very often the way we treat God! We view God as the killjoy to life. God is the one who goes and ruins our life! Really? Is that true? I don't think so!

When I go back over my life, I would say that God has given me something to live for! God has given me purpose. God has given me the vision. God has kept me on the straight and narrow. That's not a boring life. That's an exciting life because it keeps me safe from harm, safe from doing ruination to myself! It saves me from riding the wrong way down the motorway of life, keeping me out of harm's way!

God keeps us out of harm's way by giving us his law so that our life can be wonderful! It is for freedom that Christ has set us free as long as we are living according to God's rules! I hope you will enjoy that freedom on the motorway of life!

Going down the motorway the wrong way on that motorbike in India didn't bring freedom! It brought fear and unnecessary endangerment to my life and others! Just think about the decisions you are making today. What will the end result be? Will it truly be freedom for you and for the others those decisions impact? Or is it a reckless shortcut that proves to be no shortcut at all? You have a future which God has planned!

April 22nd 2021

This Comes to You with the Letter E!

Top of the morning, to ya and welcome to 'an cupán tea with the Rev!' Today's 'an cupán tae' comes to you with the letter E! That is - E for essential. And also, to add to that, it's comes to you with the verse from Joshua chapter 1:9!

In these Covid times "Essential" is the buzz word nowadays. Is your business essential? Is what you're going to do essential? Is anything essential? We can give you a letter for work because your work is essential. To buy children's shoes is essential. To buy adult shoes is not essential. As I said 'Essential' is the word!

I think it's ridiculous, partly because of the following example. During the week Queen Victoria[13] who does a lot of walking discovered that her runners were banjaxed! They were wrecked. And so as a random act of kindness. I decided I would go and buy my wife a pair of runners.

---

[13] Queen Victoria – The Rev's Wife

Off I went to the shop and I got as far as the door to be met by the security person who was actually just the shop assistant. And I said, 'can I buy this size of runner in this brand please?'

No!

No?

No. It's not essential!

Really? I said "the other ones are worn out. So are you saying that we should just walk around in our bare feet?"

The assistant replied: "If it's a child, then you need to make an appointment, you need to go and bring the child in and then you could get them. But you need an appointment, especially for a fitting, etc. But you must phone beforehand…

I said "It's not a child. It's an adult!"

"No, can't sell you anything!"

"So you're telling me it's okay for children to have shoes, but it's not okay for adults to have shoes!"

Well folks, you know, it's no wonder that we have ended up being the particular generation of persons with such a fetish about shoes, because it reminds me of yesteryear, when back in the day… well maybe this was our experience, but not yours, when you always wore the 'new shoes' that were passed down from the previous person!

And so because we were deprived of shoes, now that we have the resources we have gone mad buying shoes! But now that we are in need of shoes, you can't get them because they're 'not essential!' Madness!

But now to focus on this verse of scripture, as I get to my point on what is essential. Folks, it is essential for us to get a hold of 'what is essential!' Joshua chapter 1 and verse 9 is a very familiar passage and it reads:

> Be strong and courageous. Do not be terrified. Do not be discouraged. For the Lord your God will be with you wherever you go.

Now Joshua was someone who was seasoned. He was a man of war. And he was the one who actually led Israel. He had fought many battles at this point already. But now they're at the edge of the Promised land. Now they're about to move into what God has promised them. And here God turns up and speaks to him. Right? But you know what Joshua's like, he's a man! A real man! A man's man, as they say, and yet the Lord comes down and says to him: 'be strong and courageous!' So Joshua was obviously having some sort of an internal conflict. And in this moment he wasn't feeling strong and courageous. Why else would God show up?

Now I am one of these people who was born with skinny arms and skinny legs. You know, my father once went and said that I had knots on a piece of string for arms! You know, I had an arm with a knot on it for an elbow joint on an arm that was a piece of string! Make no mistake, he was talking about my elbows, he wasn't talking about my muscles. And do you know what else? I was one of those people that was born with skinny arms, skinny legs and a pot belly and nothing has changed since! I've just got a bit bigger!

And yet as you rightly know, most of us are not some sort of superhero or demi-god from times past or even Joshua for that matter! Or any other superhero either that may be out there. No we are just normal! And yet God is saying to us today - and it is essential that you get this - Be strong! Be courageous! Do not be afraid! Do not be discouraged!

Why? Because I'm with you! What's essential for us to get a hold of folks, is the company that we keep! For those of us who are Christians, the company that we keep is God! So let me encourage you with these words: Don't be discouraged! Don't be fearful! For this is what's essential…

God is with you!

Folks now have a great day. Have a great week. God bless and thank you for joining me for our 'cupán tae!' Oh…

By the way it says this as well in the Bible, just in passing and as it pops into my mind - that when the Israelites walked around the desert for 40 years, their shoes didn't wear out! And, their clothes didn't wear out! How come they don't make shoes like that anymore?

April 29th 2021

Look to the Birds

Hey, good morning folks and welcome to our 'an cupán tae with the Rev.' Do you know it's amazing what a little bit of sunshine can do! As I was out for my walk, heading down the road to see my few animals as I do every day, lo and behold the neighbours had all come out as the sun had arrived! There they were like meerkats, worshipping the sun!

Suddenly the sunshine comes out and everyone is there - Boom! And people are talking, happy and energized. Anyway, enough about the worship and the whole sun thing. People are out and about now in the garden, so they are up for having a chat.

Yet the main concern is worry. They're worrying about how old people are going to survive the pandemic. Sorry old people! I don't want to be accused of being ageist, but I'm just telling you how it is! There is the worry about school, worry about exams, worry about how life is going to be, worry about the rising numbers who have covid. And so everyone is talking about their worries!

And so I think it's important for us to go and dig into Matthew's Gospel this morning. Just for a quick read. The thing is that as I'm looking this up, around here I think it's beautiful. There are two buzzards outside my window and they are flying around; doing acrobatics in the air. It looks amazing the way that they can just glide and float on the wind and do all these stunts. It's like an interwoven dance in the air. Everyone says that if there are buzzers around there won't be a small bird to be seen anywhere. They're all going to be gone. The buzzards will clear the whole place out.

But the thing I have noticed in our place, it's quite the opposite. We have these two buzzers floating around the sky as I have said but the population of small birds has really grown around our area.

We always fed the little birds, but the thing is that they've multiplied in number. I actually think it's because other birds that normally steal eggs have been stopped from doing so. They're kept at bay because of these two big birds of prey that are flying around. It's like they're the sentinels, they're the guardians. And we too have two guardians looking after our lives. Psalm 23:6 says:

> Surely goodness and mercy will follow me
> all the days of my life.

Like two guardians watching us, following us, making sure that we are okay. Matthew chapter 6. Jesus states the following:

> Therefore, I tell you, do not worry about your life. What you will eat or drink or about your body, what you will wear; is not life more important than food, and the body more important than clothes? Look at the birds of the air. They do not sow or reap or store away in barns, and yet your heavenly Father feeds them. Are you not much more valuable than they?

You know what God is saying to us today? God is saying:

Stop!

Look at nature!

Look at the birds of the air!

When is the last time that you went and stopped up and you considered the little birds in your garden? Maybe you feed them out in the back. But when is it that you've actually taken time to notice them? I was sitting here in my little log cab looking out the window and at the hedge beside it. It was full of little common finches, garden finches, green finches. And they are all in there, they are busy and really industrious, but they are safely tucked away in the hedge. There they are peeping out at you and then they come out and they get their food and all that.

And God is saying to you look at them.

Look at the birds.

Consider the birds.

So, when I'm sitting at the back window of our house and watching those two buzzards swooping, flying and gliding, this is what God is saying to me:

Look at them.

I provide for all of them.

Now, if I care about the birds in this world, how much more do I care about you?

But, folks, that is what God is saying to you too! Listen as Jesus continues here in Matthew 6…

> And why do you worry about clothes? See how the lilies of the field grow, they do not labour or spin. Yet I tell you that not even Solomon in all his splendour was dressed like one of these. If that is how God clothes the grass of the field which is here today and tomorrow is thrown into the fire, will he not also clothe you? Oh you of little faith. So do not worry. What shall we eat? Or what shall we drink? Or what shall we wear? For the people of the world go after all these things and your Heavenly Father knows that you need them. But seek first His kingdom and His righteousness and all these things will be given to you as well.

So God is saying put me first. I give you clothes, I give you food, I will give you everything you need. So why worry?

Jesus continues:

> Therefore, do not worry about tomorrow. For tomorrow will worry about itself. Each day has enough trouble of its own!

So, if you're someone sitting right now in a state of worry, maybe you were never a worrywart but the circumstances you find yourself in now have made you one. Chuck your worry out! God's got you! After all, Jesus says that you are more valuable than these little birds! God is saying that:

You are important to Him.

You are of worth to Him.

You are someone that is special to Him.

So, please don't lose focus on who you are and don’t lose focus on who is holding you! Hey, don't worry about a thing, every little thing is going to be alright. So don't worry…

You get the drift. Have a good week and chat to you soon. God's got you!

May 6th 2021

Soaking in Grace!

Hello and welcome to 'an cupántae with the Rev!' The very fact that you are reading this means that you didn't wake up dead this morning!

WOO HOO! YOU'RE ALIVE!

Oh folks, I tell you one thing - I'm discovering I'm getting old. And here's one of the clues that I'm getting old, I'm starting to remember, to reminisce all the time. I remember when…

But one of the things I have been thinking about is how God has gone out of our conversation, other than using Jesus' name as a swear word. Think about it. Here's a little challenge for you for the day or whenever it is that you read this. A little challenge for you. Check out the number of times that a person goes and says something like 'God bless you!' or 'By God's grace…' Or 'God willing…' or 'there but for the grace of God go I...'

So as your day progresses, see how many times God is referenced because I remember there was a time when that was the norm. People would end their statements with 'God willing' or 'by God's grace I was able to' or 'God love us all!' But these are gone. No one appears to use these statements anymore.

So that's the challenge. See how many people actually mention the word God. Take note of it. How often do they mention the word 'God' or 'God bless you.' or 'God keep you' Or any of those God sayings that used to be floating around all the time when you were a child.

If you were going to come along to any Methodist church service, we finish worship with something that is called 'The Grace' which is actually the benediction, a closing prayer, a closing blessing which says:

> May the grace of our Lord Jesus Christ and the love of God and the fellowship of the Holy Spirit be with you all now and evermore. Amen.

That is taken straight from Scripture, straight from 2 Corinthians chapter 13:14. And I was just thinking about the topic of God's grace.

It's by God's grace you're awake today.

It's by God's grace you're alive.

It's by God's grace that you are here to enjoy this world.

It is by God's grace that you can enjoy His favour.

It is by God's grace that you are able to work.

It's by God's grace that you have the health that you have. It is by God's grace that you have the food that you have. Everything is by the grace of God!

And we just kind of trivialise it, we seem to have come to a point where we're wondering: what is God's grace anyway? We just bandy the term about, and yet God is gracious to you. God is gracious to me.

It's great. Here I am. It's a nice morning this morning. I'm just back from my walk and I just… Now hold on, hold on. I know what you think: 'Oh, well, he's a Methodist minister. It's alright for him going walking around. He has loads of time while the rest of us are working!'

Well, let me tell you something. While I was working in the Tyre Shop a decade ago, believe it or not, I was running around the roads, training for my first marathon. And if you don't believe that, Google it! You'll find me… Dingle Marathon in 2012! I did my first Half Marathon in 2011.

And as I reflect on those morning runs, you know it's unreal the blessing of God. But also as I look back over those 10 years. I can trace God's blessing, God's favour, God's goodness, God sustaining me, God helping me.

So what I want to say today is that you are someone who is blessed by the grace of God - as you are! As I said, if you woke up this morning and found yourself alive, you are blessed!

You know, I haven't got to the point where I'm old enough yet to just go and stick on the radio. You know, people who do this, stick on the radio and the first thing they do is listen to the obituaries, and when they discover that their name is not on it, they know they're still around and they can go: "Woo Hoo! we have the day to face now. Things are looking up. I'm not dead. They didn't report me dead on the radio!

Yes, I know I am not that far yet. I'm living. I'm alive. I'm someone who's blessed. Someone who's enjoying the year of God's favour. Someone who is soaking in God's wondrous grace to me!

So folks, may the grace of our Lord Jesus Christ and the love of God and the fellowship of the Holy Spirit be with us all now and forever more. Amen. I'm hoping that you're enjoying your day. Blessed in the grace of God! Enjoy your old cup of tea and just sit back and think about it. But remember that challenge. Keep an ear out! Listen to how many people come into your day and say these sort of phrases: 'God bless you,' 'By God's grace.,' 'God willing,' 'But for the grace of God,' 'Thank God.'

I think it is time that we revive those sayings. And remember the goodness of God in our everyday lives. May the grace of the Lord Jesus Christ… The grace of His… His grace - what a word. We are a favoured people living in the grace of God! Soaking in His Grace – what a privilege - AMEN!

May 13th 2021

Learning to Be…

Oh Boy, that's a rough one out there! But sure tis time for our 'an cupán tae!' Goodness me, the old hair has gone mad due to the wind and rain out there! But that's a day that you wouldn't put the wheel of a bike out! I tell you the ducks are even taking the day off! You know the way people here in Ireland would say when it's raining' it's a day for the ducks! Well I tell you tis no day for the ducks! Now back in the days when I worked on the buildings they would say on a day like that, it was a "day for the high stool or a day for the fire!"

All that aside folks, the scripture that has been buzzing around my brain since the last time we spoke is Paul writing in the book of Philippians. He says that he learned to be content in all circumstances. And here is what it actually says in Philippians 4:10-13 just to put the verse in context –

> I rejoice greatly in the Lord that at last you have renewed your concern for me. Indeed, you have been concerned, but you had no opportunity to show it. I am not saying this because I am in need, for I have learned to be content whatever the circumstances. I know what it is to be in need. I know what it is to have plenty. I have learned the secrets to being content in any and every situation, whether well fed or hungry, whether living in plenty or in want. I can do all this through him who gives me strength.

Now there's that famous verse which people love to go and

quote, 'I can do all things through Christ who strengthens me.' But that's not the verse I want to look at. The verse I want to think about today is 'I have learned to be content in all circumstances' as the reality is that our world feeds on discontent. As soon as you put on the TV, every advert is talking about discontent! You need a new car. You need this new appliance. You need this product or that gadget!

But the advert that really upsets me is the one at Christmas where they put out this big spread of food saying this is the time for the family gathering and you and we all will have a wonderful time! But the truth is that's not what the average Christmas looks like! Who has a Christmas like that? But you know, we have all been sold this ideal. If you have a Christmas spread like this, then your life will be perfect!

The result? A seed of discontent has been sown. So we walk around all day thinking 'one day I could earn enough money and I'll get that, or if only I could do this, or if only I had that, or if only I had this other thing!' And so our thought process 24 hours a day becomes…Oh, if only, if only, if only, if only, if only, if only, if only, IF ONLY…

Ohhh… I tell you one thing. If only you went and stood outside now for a second you'd be freezing with a nice cold shower! A friend went and said this morning on Facebook, 'How come it's November? did I miss the summer?' Really? Did you not hear the saying 'a wet and windy May fills the haggard full of hay?' Do you know what folks, you look out the window today and guess what, our seasons are back on track? This is what it's supposed to be like in May!

Last year we were suffering from the drought with the lack of rain at this time of year! We are never content about the weather either.

So back to contentment! Here's the thing… 'I have learned to be content in all circumstances' - I actually believe that when we become content it isn't that we have suddenly backed off. It isn't something that we've lost our enthusiasm to want to achieve. What's actually going on is it actually frees us up to achieve even greater things because we're no longer consumed with ourselves and our own issues! We have now got time to be there for everyone else, to be able to do things for other people.

Even our dog is outside giving out about the weather, and the duck is out there giving out about the weather! They can both go on about the weather though what they're giving out about I don't know. They're not content either!

So how can we be content? Paul says there is a secret to this contentment. Where can we find the secret? It is found in Proverbs and chapter 19! Now, this is something I really think is very exciting! Proverbs 19:23 says this:

> The fear of the Lord leads to life; then one rests content untouched by trouble.

Folks, the fear of the Lord leads to life; then one rests content, untouched by trouble - I hope you can go and say that that's where your life is at!

I said now, contentment, being content frees you up to be able to do things for other people. John Wesley went and gave the following rule for Christian living. See how you fair out…

> Do all the good you can,
> By all the means you can,
> By all the ways you can,
> In all the places you can,
> And all the times you can,
> To all the people you can,
> As long as ever you can.

So what have you got to be content about? Start praising God! But if you are someone suffering from being discontented, well you know the answer!

May 20th 2021

Trouble Free…?

Ah how is it going? Sure folks I am like a dog chasing his tail these days and sure there is no catching it at all. Running around in circles and nothing to show for it. And yes, added to that, I'm late for my 'an cupán tae' by a whole day whoa! Folks, I have just been having a crazy week, and now I'm like a greyhound let out of a trap. I'm racing I am! Racing from deadline to deadline at the present minute.

But here's the thing, last week when I was thinking about the verse of Scripture that we were sharing and I was reflecting on it, just to bring you up to speed, I had spoken about Paul and that he had learned to be content in all circumstances. We know that the circumstances he found himself in were all crazy circumstances. And then I quoted the verse from Proverbs chapter 19:23 and I'll just read it here to you:

> The fear of the Lord leads to life, then
>
> one rests content untouched by trouble.

And it occurred to me that when you hear that verse your reaction could be 'Yeah right, well we all know that's not true. We all suffer from troubles and grief and hassle!'

But this verse isn't promising a trouble-free life. This verse is promising that in the midst of your troubles you can be content, you can rest contentedly. And so as Christians, when we face bad news, when we end up hearing something we don't want to hear, be it illness, or a phone call, as in our case many years back when suddenly our house was on fire, or when you end up in a car crash, or in some other unexpected event - you can still rest content in the Lord. So maybe you're someone going through a bad time, you're going through a rough time, and the last thing you need to hear is that a Christian life is one where you can be trouble-free and that you don't have to have any hassles or problems! But that's not what God is saying. God has never said that. And if you take the time to read Bible stories, you'll discover that that has never been God's promise. What God is saying or teaching us, is that we can be content in the knowledge that He is with us.

So that fear, the verse speaks of means that we have respect for God. Part of the outworking of that is that you are inviting God into your everyday. Your expectation is that life can and will only be able to get on some sort of even keel if God is involved. Then, even if troubles come, because God is with you, you have nothing to fear, you can rest content. Troubles come and troubles go, and some troubles can be fairly permanent and fairly serious.

You may be someone who has gone through a personal calamity, or maybe you're going through a personal calamity, Or it may be worse than that, you may know that the diagnosis is not good going forward. But what is God saying in this scripture? He is saying you can still rest content. And that is the meaning of this statement in Philippians 4:7:

> The peace of God, which transcends all understanding, will guard your hearts and your minds in Christ Jesus.

This suddenly makes complete sense!

When the 'normal' reaction is that you should be jumping up and down, losing the rag and going crazy and being completely freaked out by the circumstances you find yourself in, you find that in the midst of that craziness, you can rest content, you have a peace that passes all understanding. It's not a super spiritual sort of thing, it's not an inward peace sort of thing, it's not by focusing one's mind or some other psychological trick you're playing on yourself – No!

The source of that peace is God! And, so even in the midst of all the hurry and racing, I needed to stop up for this quick cup of tea with you just to say "Hey guys, do you know that verse I went and mentioned last week? It doesn't mean that you're going to live without trouble. But what it does mean is that in the midst of your trouble you can rest content... And here is the reason why…

THE LORD IS WITH YOU!

June 4th 2021

Thermometers and Thermostats

Welcome to 'an cupán tea with the Rev.' And guys, today, this is about my incubator, my new toy. And so I'm experimenting. But there's something that really struck me about this which I just want to share with you. I thought this very interesting. And in fairness, it's not the first time that I've heard this, and I'm sure it's not the first time that you've heard it either that there are two types of people in the world. There are people who are thermostats and people who are thermometers.

Now, this machine has both and if you turn the little screw on the thermostat one way or the other, it'll definitely affect everything. And so when it comes to people and there being two types of people, the 'thermometer' is someone that just lets you know the way things are.

The function of the thermometer on the incubator is simply to let you know that this incubation chamber is continuously at 100 degrees Fahrenheit. If it was Celsius, the eggs would be baked. Anyway, it is 100 degrees

Fahrenheit. And so that's its job. It just goes and tells you where things are at. And so you have people just like that. That's what they do. They're always telling you the way things are. There are no solutions, no anything, and they will just talk about it all day long, always just talking about the way things are.

The thermostat, however, regulates things. It impacts things. So the people who are thermostats, are the people who make an impact. They make a marked difference on the whole situation. So just like the little thermostat operated by this screw on the incubator, if you twist it one way, it brings the temperature down, but if you twist it the other way, it brings the temperature up. They also actually affect the climate of our world.

With the incubator at the right temperature set up through the thermostat by God's grace, hopefully, we will end up with little chickens coming out of the eggs, fulfilling the function I got it for in the first place. And there are people like that as well who make a difference in our world, moulding it and shaping it.

Now there's another thing that you can see regarding the thermometer; it's visible. There's no problem seeing it. It is out there. Sticking out like a sore thumb, as obvious as the nose on your face, but the thermostat can't be seen. And very often, the person who makes the big changes and the waves in this world goes unnoticed and unseen. That's just something to think about.

But what if there was someone who expects us, all of us, to go and impact our world, not just to be thermometers, not just to be ones who are reflecting on the way society is, but like thermostats genuinely making a difference. Could it not be said that indeed God is the one who is expecting us to make an impact, to make a difference to society?

Now the way that God has asked us to make a difference is through two commands. Firstly, to love the Lord our God with all our heart, mind, soul and strength and secondly to love our neighbour as ourselves. And sometimes that sounds very theoretical, very grandiose, super-spiritual even and we can be left wondering how to put this into practice.

In Romans 12 Paul talks about how our minds have to be transformed which is what the thermostat actually does. It goes and transforms the environment.

> Therefore, I urge your brothers and sisters in the view of God's mercy to offer your bodies as a living sacrifice, holy and pleasing to God - this is your true and proper worship. Do not conform to the pattern of this world, but be transformed by the renewing of your mind. Then you will be able to test and approve what God's will is - His good pleasing and perfect will.
>
> Romans 2:1-3

There's the love of God and how you are to relate to the Lord your God with all your heart, mind, soul and strength. But if we just jump down a little bit in the same chapter, we're given a very practical way of how we can be a thermostat in our world. Let's look at that list found in Romans 12:9-21…

> Love must be sincere. Hate what is evil, cling to what is good. Be devoted to one another in love. Honour one another above yourselves. Never be lacking in zeal, but

keep your spiritual fervour in serving the Lord. Be joyful in hope, patient in affliction, faithful in prayer. Share with the Lord's people who are in need. Practice hospitality. Bless those who persecute you, bless and do not curse. Rejoice with those who rejoice; mourn with those who mourn. Live in harmony with one another. Do not be proud, but be willing to associate with people of low position. Do not be conceited. Do not repay anyone evil for evil. Be careful to do what is right in the eyes of everyone. If it is possible and as far as it depends on you, live in peace with everyone. Do not take revenge, my dear friends, but leave room for God's wrath. For it is written, it is mine to avenge, I will repay, says the Lord. On the contrary, if your enemy is hungry, feed him. If he is thirsty, give him something to drink. In doing this you will heap burning coals on his head. Do not be overcome by evil, but overcome evil with good.

Now there is a very practical list of how it is that you and I can be a thermostat in our world. So here is the challenge… who are you? Are you someone who is just echoing what society is, like the thermometer? Simply noting the temperature of the current cultural context in which you live, just telling me the way things are? Or are you a thermostat, one who is regulating that temperature, regulating the environment that you are a part of?

But if you are a thermostat what impact, what imprint are you making on the world around you and is that impact for God? Interesting question, isn't it? Two types of people in the world. So who are you?

June 11th 2021

The End of a Nine Year Journey

Howdy folks and welcome to this 'an Cupán Tae with the Rev.' It's Friday morning, the 11th of June 2021 and this is almost like a little blog that you're joining me on today. I only tell you that to let you know that what I would like to share with you this morning is a story of God's goodness and grace and adventure with God.

So often I think as Christians we just go around with the weight of thc world on our shoulders. I'm not saying that I'm not one of those people but the thing is that today is one of the last two days of a nine-year adventure. The last two days of one journey and the commencement of another.

So what has actually taken place that has taken me nine years? Well tomorrow evening I'm going to be ordained as a Methodist minister. It was never my intention to become a Methodist Minister. As you all know, I was working as a floor manager in a Tyre shop. But this whole adventure started nine years ago when I was approached by Rev. Bill and asked if I would consider ministry. Well the truth is I had never considered being a minister in the church, and yet God had just gone and opened a door for me. It's been amazing. I would just like to share with you how amazing it has been.

Sometimes we think that God works in a really slow way or that He's not involved at all. You could say nine years, that's a long time and yes, it is a long time but it's been a crazy adventure. So just to let you know as a person who is very simple in faith, I just trust the Lord. You mightn't agree with me but that is the truth, and so when I was actually approached by Rev. Bill in regard to considering ordained ministry, I prayed a simple little prayer and this was my prayer:

> 'Lord, as long as the door stays open I'll stay walking. If this is the journey you're taking me on then I'll stay walking'

Well folks, there were plenty of opportunities where that door could have closed. God could have shut the door but what I'm saying is, I was not going to be the one who would shut the door. I intended to be faithful in walking where the Lord wanted me to walk and there's a relevant scripture here in Revelation 3:8…

> Look I have set before you an open door which no one is able to shut. I know you have but little power and yet you've kept my word and not denied my name.

When I look at that verse and look back with hindsight I can see the truth of that. When the Lord took me on this journey or started taking me on this journey we had just come out of the circumstance of our house burning down. It was about a year or so after our house had been burnt down, and that event was a kind of reset button in some ways. I was in a very tired place. I was in a weary place and the last thing I was thinking about was Christian anything other than just maintaining my relationship with the Lord.

So becoming a minister in a church was definitely the last thing I was thinking about. It hadn't even crossed my radar and so that's why it took someone like Rev Bill to come up and say "I think you should consider this".

So here I am after stepping out in a simple way with a simple prayer on a journey that has been nine years. I'm just about ready, the car is packed ready to hit the road and head off for the ordination service. At this point I want to thank you, I want to thank all of you that have been involved in this journey.

Even in the last two years because of the way the Methodist church works you are a probationary minister for two years. So I've been a minister with an L plate around my neck for the last two years and now the Lord is bringing that journey to a close. But as that journey comes to a close who knows what the Lord's got in store.

All I want to tell you though is that the last nine years have been such an adventure, it's been crazy what God has been doing. Absolutely amazing what God has been doing and such a blessed time! So I just want to thank all who have been involved in this journey, especially my Tyre shop family who were there for me through many of those years, and also all the churches I've been posted to in the last two years and the churches that have been there as I have been going through my practicals etc, etc.

Also to all the rest of the congregations and the ministers that have been involved in that journey - guys a sincere thank you. You've all blessed me. It's just been amazing and I'm overcome with emotion. God is a great God, folks, a great God, and you can live in the same house, in the same place, not move anywhere and have a life that's full of adventure and fun in the Lord and that's just what I want to say in this little 'an cupán tae.'

June 17th 2021

As a Hen…

Welcome to this 'an cupán tae wth the Rev.' Folks, I just wanted to let you know I'm super-excited. Do you remember a few weeks back I was talking to you about my new toy when I was using the incubator. Well I have had three little chicks come out. But then, Queen Victoria had this wonderful plan to go and put the three chicks under a hen that had been wanting to hatch.

And so the hen has become the adoptive parent of these three chicks. Now I wanted to show you my three chicks because it's really exciting. There are so many things buzzing around in my head just in regard to the whole process and how that relates to God and how it relates to Scripture. And so I wanted to show you my three chicks with their new Mum. But alas you will just have to picture them in your mind.

Anyway, no hen was harmed in the process but my green shovel was! There I was trying to feed them and you see the hen is super-protective and attacked my little shovel. Right away you know the Scriptures jumping into your head which Jesus said as He was riding into Jerusalem. When He saw Jerusalem He said He longed to gather Jerusalem like a hen gathers its chicks under its wings. And so here you have this hen and she has gathered the chicks under her wings. She was not going to let me go near those chicks and attacked my trowel.

This gives us a sense of just how protective God is. Just imagine how much God loves you and protects you. And the Scripture goes and speaks about that in Proverbs 18:10 that:

> The name of the Lord is a strong tower the righteous run to it and they are safe.

This verse speaks about how God is our protection. That God is our security. That God is our shield. In fact there are so many Scriptures that connect with the image of Jesus as our Lord longing to protect us. So as we consider this simple little demonstration of this hen gathering her chicks, we can see the impact of Jesus's words when He's speaking about Jerusalem. But Paul writes in Colossians 3:2-3:

> Set your mind on things above not on earthly
> things. For you died and your life is now hidden with Christ in God.

'You died' simply means that since you have become a Christian you've died to earthly things. Now I know I've touched on that before, but what a picture that your life has been hidden with Christ in God. God is the one who is surrounding you, protecting you.

Now I was going to try and move the hen with my little shovel so I wouldn't be attacked because I had been feeding the chicks in the incubator before moving them to their new adoptive mother. I was checking if they were ok but as soon as I did that the hen just started bristling up straight away. She was ready to launch an attack! And not once were those little chicks revealed.

So here's the thing that I think is exciting: Here in nature God gives us a picture of His love and protection for you. But also the other little picture that comes out of that, which I think is brilliant, is it brings out in Galatians and in Ephesians that we have been adopted. God has adopted us to be His sons and daughters. And my hen has adopted these chicks as her own. These were not her chicks.

In the passage of scripture Jesus says that as a hen gathers her chicks - but my hen isn't gathering her chicks - she is gathering her adopted chicks under her wings. These chicks have become hers. And so what we're seeing is a similar picture in the spiritual realm of how God has adopted us, protects us, and He has taken the rights of a parent over us. He has become our parent and that's why we call him father. And that's why he protects, loves and cherishes us. Isn't that a beautiful little picture?

Just from the time this hen of Queen Victoria's has adopted those three little chicks we have seen that hen gathering those chicks under her wings. How protective that hen has become over her chicks. And in all these things we see that God loves, protects, adopts and cares for us. What a picture!

I will probably have another chicken story for you next week because of these three little chicks, but it's amazing just what has taken place here in the natural that fills us with understanding of what God has done for us in the spiritual. Anyway have a wonderful blessed and glorious week as you know that you are loved, protected and cherished by our Heavenly Father. God Bless.

June 24th 2021

Up and Running…

Good morning and welcome to 'an cupán tae with the Rev'. Well I said to you I'd be back with another chicken story. My three little chicks are looking good. Well the thing that I want to share with you today is this, or rather the question I want to ask you is this: what is your passion? What drives you? What excites you? What gets you going?

So often especially when you are my age in the middle years of life and you're suddenly providing for your kids and you have the mortgage and you have all these other things you can tend to lose your passions and desires. We tend to end up with life becoming humdrum. That's the word. Humdrum. Just the same old, same old.

But that's not the case, guys. One of the things that really excites me about my little chicks is, they wake up, they come out of the egg, they chip away, and they chip away, and they chip away until out of the egg they come. But unlike anything else, they hit the ground running, they're up, they just dry themselves off and they're away.

Then they're up and they're going around the place really fast chirping away and exploring the world. But the fact that they hit the ground running fascinates me.

If a calf is born there's a period of time where the mother goes and licks it and cleans it and dries it and gets it all excited and then encourages it to get up onto its feet, and then it has to get a blast of milk before it's ready to step into living life. Lambs are the same. I reared little budgies before and the mother there is busy feeding the babies every day all the time and the father is feeding the mother. It's a beautiful picture as well. It still takes a period of time before the birds are ready to leave the nest but that's a different story for a different day.

But not the chicken. It comes out of its egg and it's up and ready, it's going, it's looking for food, it's looking for water, it's moving, it's cracking on with life and that's the thing I find inspiring. Just as that chick comes out of the egg, looking, searching, seeking food and here they are a few weeks later and they're still going around the place. The hen is there and she's encouraging them, speaking to them, chatting to them the whole time. They're all busy, busy, busy, so enthusiastic, not a moment to lose, frenetic unbelievable activity.

So the question I want to put to you is: where is your passion? What fires you up? What enthuses you? What do you get up for in the morning? Or have you become a slave to the humdrum? Have you lost the passion of that little chicken? You see the thing is that when they grow up to become hens and we let them out of their hen house and all that stuff, they're still out there scratching. They're busy, they're rooting, they're occupied, and they have a hunger and thirst to find their food, their water and they're busy out doing it.

Now in a spiritual sense my prayer is that we will be like those little chicks. When we come out of the egg that is in regard to your spiritual walk with Christ, this time being born again… BOOM, there you are, and you want to go and find food. Now the place we find our spiritual food is in God's Word, the Bible and the one we go to looking for our spiritual living water is the Spirit of God who is living within us as we know from John chapter 4. It's a story well worth reading if you don't know it.

Now here's the scripture that the little chick reminds me of in Psalm 63:1

> Oh God you are my God, earnestly I seek you, my soul thirsts for you, my flesh faints for you as in a dry and weary land where there is no water.

So if you profess to be a follower of Jesus Christ, a Christian, irrespective of where you worship, let me ask you this: Would you describe yourself in this way?

When you wake up in the morning, are you like that little chick, up and running, and is your first thought God, flying around in your mind? You are my God, I earnestly seek you–like that little chick who gets up and earnestly seeks his food. He's seeking nourishment, he's seeking to be built up and edified in his physical body and so too we should be the same as we earnestly seek God. Let us look again at Psalm 63:1-3

> Oh God you are my God, earnestly I seek you, my soul thrusts for you, my flesh faints for you as in a dry and weary land where there is no water. So I have looked upon you in the sanctuary beholding your power

> and glory because your lovingkindness is better than life. My lips will praise you.

Folks, you are probably reading these little stories and you are thinking Nigel never has a dull day. Well that's not true! This last week I've been going through a few dull days. A bit of a dull time but the Lord has ministered and spoken to me beautifully, and this is one of the moments I'm sharing with you, how he's ministered to me. Let's not get distracted by the things of life, let's not become enslaved to the humdrum, let's not go there, this is another day, another scenario, another opportunity to rejoice, for this is the day the Lord has made, and we have reason to rejoice and be glad in it. Let us earnestly seek Him.

Talk to you soon! Be encouraged to be like the little chick, up and running and going for it. God bless you.

July 1st 2021

Eternal

I have, according to my sister, become another year older but not necessarily any wiser. Ah well, don't you love it when people send nice words of encouragement like that! but I also got a really cool birthday present. Look what I got… a mug with this inscription 'Is maith liom cupán tae'. Apparently, a supermarket chain has actually come to realize that this little weekly 'an cupán tae' session has become such a great thing that they have actually produced their own mug range.

Anyway, thank you to my mother-in-law, Elsie, for this beautiful little birthday present. 'Is maith liom 'cupán tae' means 'I like a cup of tea' for those of you who need a translation. Now one more chicken story I want to tell all you guys.

Well maybe there will be more, I don't know, as these little talks are based just on things that really excite or inspire me. So, I'm outside here in the sun and you can hear the hens all making noise. In fact, everything is making noise around the place but let's not worry about that. One more good little chicken story. What happens is that when the little chickens are in the coop with the mother hen, the mother hen is continuously talking to them going cluck, cluck, cluck, cluck, cluck, cluck, cluck, cluck, all the time going around talking to the little chickens and it's just 'continuous encouragement, continuous reassurance, continuous reminders that I'm there for you.' And that really got me thinking, that really got me excited.

You know there's a lot made nowadays of mental health and about being encouraging and being supportive and all that sort of stuff. And the thing is it's nothing new, that's the gas thing about it, it's nothing new. This is something that God has been doing all the time. And I love this little verse in 2 Thessalonians 2:16-17:

> May our Lord Jesus Christ Himself and God our Father who loved us and by His grace gave us eternal encouragement and good hope.

Notice the word gave, it’s past tense. In other words, it's not that he's giving, it's not that he will give, he has already given us eternal encouragement. And I love that. That means that just like the hen is continuously encouraging and reassuring her little chicks and talking to the Lord, God is encouraging you. God is encouraging me all the time. Eternal. Never ending. Continuous encouragement. God has given us continuous encouragement.

But do you know, one of the things that is very, very popular nowadays, when you go and talk about God with anyone, - the first thing that they would say is, if God exists today, how could he let things like this or that happen? But here's the thing, I believe the problem is we're not listening. We are not listening to what God is saying. That's it.

Nature we are told speaks to the world. Creation is the biblical word used. Creation speaks forth knowledge of God all the time. But this isn't just about what we see around us speaking of God but also what we observe speaks of God such as my little hen and her three chicks that she adopted a few weeks back and has been encouraging ever since. So we're looking at a natural picture which goes and describes how wonderful God is in his encouragement to you and me. Eternal encouragement.

Now here's an observation. If you have a relationship with God and you're not hearing encouraging words from God, well, I would say that's because you're not listening. Yeah, that's what I said. I think you're not listening. Now how do we listen?

Well, one of the ways that we listen to what God has got to say is we read God's word, the Bible. And that's where we're getting this little 'an cupán tae' from each week and discovering God's eternal encouragement from Scripture. Now let's look at the verses again from 2 Thessalonians as I got a little carried away and didn't finish reading them all

> May our Lord Jesus Christ Himself and God our Father, who loved us and by His grace gave us eternal encouragement and good hope, encourage your hearts and strengthen you in every good deed and word.

God's intent is that by His eternal encouragement, like my hen talking to her chicks all the time, He wants you to be ENCOURAGED in your heart and STRENGTHENED in every good deed and word. So let me ask you the question, are you encouraged today? Are you encouraged by what God is saying to you today? Or are you hearing anything at all?

'You're going on a bit Nigel! We know you're into all this stuff.' 'No, no, no, I'm not into all this stuff. I'm telling you that God is encouraging you. God is encouraging me. All we need to be doing is making sure that we're listening.'

'Oh, yeah. I disagree with my sister, by the way. You know, her words aren't very encouraging. I am wiser, whatever about being older. So come on, let's be real. Until next week, guys, be encouraged. Listen to that eternal encouragement. Take care. Till next week, God bless.'

July 15th 2021

Life, Have You Got It?

I woke up this morning! Woooohoooo! 'Welcome to 'an cupán tae.' Okay, I get it, I hear you. I know what you're saying. There's no need for that sort of sarcasm. It's just not nice, it's not doing you any credit! There is no need for the 'oh well done there, Sherlock. You've figured out that you're awake this morning and that you woke up. Woohoo! Good for you.' That's not fair at all.

Anyway, what I was saying is that I woke up this morning and sometimes when I waken in the morning, my spirit is already in song. It's singing and today was one of those days when I awoke to my spirit already being in song. Singing some hymn that has just come to my mind. And this morning, the hymn, the words of the hymn, or rather the chorus of the hymn that really was speaking to me is:

> Life, life eternal life.
>
> Jesus alone is the giver.
>
> Life, life abundant life.
>
> Glory to Jesus forever.

And so that was my waking thought. And I know that I'm singing in my spirit because if I was singing physically when I woke up, I think I would awaken to a sharp, sudden pain in my side where something like an elbow might have been involved. So therefore I was most definitely singing in my spirit!

Anyway, it got me thinking of a passage of Scripture and about how wonderful life is. Now life isn't measured by your possessions. It isn't measured by your wealth. It isn't measured by how comfortable it is. Life is measured by your relationship with Jesus Christ as the chorus says, "Life, life eternal life. Jesus alone is the giver." Now I just want to share the other words of the hymn with you.

And if this describes you, then this hymn, this little talk, this 'an cupán tae,' everything today then is for you. Here are the lyrics…

Under the burden of guilt and care,

Many a soul is grieving.

Who in the joy of the Lord might

Share life everlasting receiving?

Life, life eternal life.

Jesus alone is the giver.

Life, life, abundant life,

Glory to Jesus forever.

Burdened one, why will you longer bear

Sorrows from which he releases?

Open your heart and rejoicing share

Life more abundant in Jesus.

Then there's this beautiful little picture in the next verse, a scene that we all know of…

Leaving the mountain, the streamlet grows,

Flooding the vale with a river.

So from the hill of the cross there flows,

Life more abundant forever.

Then the final verse breaks out into a prayer…

O for the floods on the thirsty land,
O for a mighty revival,
O for a sanctified fearless band,
Ready to hail its arrival.

Life, life eternal life,
Jesus alone is the giver.
Life, life, abundant life,
Glory to Jesus forever.

You know, I think that one of the things that turns people off Christians, and then as a result, Christianity, and as a result, Christ, is the long, sad, dreary disposition of most Christians. Or the way that Christians go round with the weight of the world on their shoulders. You know, somebody who professes to be a follower of Christ, may miss the experience of abundant life. In John 10 Jesus was speaking of himself as the good shepherd, and He states in John 10: 7-10:

> I tell you the truth, I am the gate for the sheep, all who ever came before me were thieves and robbers, but the sheep did not listen to them. I am the gate; whoever enters through me will be saved. He will come in and go out and find pasture. The thief comes only to steal and kill and destroy, but I have come that they may have life and have it to the full (or abundantly).

Now I am one of those people that have a natural disposition, which is not, you know, grinning, happy or smiley. As you may know this face is made for grinning, but I am happy on the inside. However, the passage talks about thieves and robbers and very often the main thief or robber, people like to suggest is Satan. Satan is the one who takes and kills and steals and all the rest of it, which he does, but we have already two other enemies of our souls, and they are the world around us and ourselves.

When we consider 'the world' I mean, have you had your daily diet of negativity today? Have you listened to the news yet? Because as soon as you switch that media source on, you are accessing your daily diet of negativity. And then you wonder why you are not happy, why the weight of the world is on your shoulders, and as you listen to all of the world's problems and start taking on the world's problems, suddenly conversation is all about the problems of the world, and then you expect to be happy?! Come on, Really?

So here's the thing, the other enemy as you know is yourself. Now let's be real. Very often the greatest enemy we have is ourselves. We put ourselves down, we feel low about ourselves, we can be very negative. Not really believing in what or who we are in Christ. Jesus says that he is the one who brings abundant life but your reaction may be something like this: 'Yeah right! Whatever you think yourself, but I haven't seen it.'

So, what I'm saying is that, as I already mentioned, it doesn't matter about your possessions, it doesn't matter about where life is at the present minute, what matters is inside. What matters is your spirit. Where is your spirit? Is your spirit soaring from the mountaintops? Is your spirit like that stream coming down the mountain growing and growing and growing?

Is it that you are a person who thinks about life, and you know you are living life to the full? You just know, and so when you are lying in bed and you wake up in the morning, a chorus like:

> Life, life eternal life,
> Jesus alone is the giver.
> Life, life, abundant life,
> Glory to Jesus forever.[14]

is on your heart. It is in your spirit, and you are filled to overflowing with hymns and songs. David actually says that the Lord ministers to us through the watches of the night. Stop! Stop looking at all the stuff around you. Stop looking at the world. Stop looking at all the negativity. I'm not saying that we should be clueless about what's going on, but have a break from that diet of daily negativity and

---

[14] Quotations taken from the hymn by W. Leslie - Under the burden of guilt and care

start thinking about what Christ has done for you. Maybe it will put a smile in your face. Abundant life, folks. Here's to it. It's found in Jesus. Have a blessed and wonderful week.

July 22nd 2021

Good – What Does That Mean?

How's it going and welcome to 'an cupán tae.' Well, I hope those of you who love sunshine are enjoying this weather because it's fairly warm outside. There's no need for me to go and give you a warm welcome this morning because you're already no doubt sweating like mad.

But, I tell you what the problem is for me this week. I'm lamenting the death of language. You see, it started way back many, many moons ago when we were in school and learning about early forms of writing. Teachers spoke of the cavemen drawing pictures on the walls of the caves and we were all looking down our noses at how primitive, how pathetic they were at drawing those pictures.

But you know what, society isn't getting much better now. They say a picture is equal to a thousand words, so I tell you what, instead of me writing any words I will just send an emoji! Yes, a happy face or a sad face. But how can you put a thousand words into a happy face? Someone probably has already done it, but come on, then you're reading something into the happy face.

When I was a teenager and I was going to a church in the last millennium, there was an elderly gentleman there. He used to say regularly that people don't know language. They don't know the roots of words, they don't understand the words that they're speaking and this was back before all the electronics and stuff that have taken over. Long before emojis for that matter!

I don't know, maybe I'm getting old, maybe I'm turning into him, I don't know. Well, you see, I've been pondering this a lot lately… communication and using words. And today the word that I'm thinking about is the word 'good' because the scripture that really has impacted me the last couple of days is Psalm 136:1

Give thanks to the Lord for He is good.

Now way back, I went and did a little talk on this on our 'an cupán tae' session: Taste and see that the Lord is good. And I said in that little piece, that it's a fact, the Psalmist gives us a fact, the Lord is good. It's up to us to taste and see.

But what does the word good mean? That's the question, isn't it? What do you understand the word good to mean? Because your understanding of the word good puts a colouring on this. That's the picture then you have of God. You know, if you walk on the road and a neighbour spots you and goes: 'Ahh, how is it going?' You respond with, 'Good!' Yeah, yeah, yeah, all's good. Good, thanks. Good. That's the same as saying fine or everything's okay or Ah, grand, thanks.

What it's basically saying is, I'm okay, but don't really ask me any more questions, end of story, go and put the topic to bed! When we talk about good, we express it in behavioural terms, 'Your behaviour was very good'. Or, 'well, your performance was good, but you could do better.' How many times have you said that? That was a good effort. And so it kind of downplays the meaning of the word. Good isn't put in the category of excellent, or what is magnificent. That was awesome. No, no, no, it was just good.

So when you come to God, you read a statement like,

> Give thanks for the Lord is good

and you're just going, yeah, good. Okay, the Lord is good. Could be better, I suppose!

Really? So I've decided that I'm just going to share this thought with you. Just wanted you to think about this. So remember, we're giving thanks for the Lord is good. This is what an old fashioned book known as the Pocket Oxford English Dictionary says that the word good means. Let's ponder on this as we have our 'an cupán tae' and consider who God is. The word good means: Commendable, Worthy, Morally excellent, Virtuous, Kind, Benevolent, Competent, Efficient, Reliable, Safe, Valid. Give thanks to the Lord for he is good. He is morally excellent. He is virtuous. He is kind. He is benevolent. He is efficient. He is competent. He is reliable. He is safe. He is valid. So when you read the word good, are they the words that come to mind in your definition? When you think of the Lord, is that how you view him? If so, then maybe you have reason to give thanks, for the Lord is good. After all this, do have a good week.

July 29th 2021

What's Your Story?

Welcome to our 'an cupán tae with the Rev,' folks. I'm just back from a few days off on various walking trips and one of those was through the Gap of Dunloe. As it says on TripAdvisor…

> A step back into time past… a good experience

We were walking along the Gap of Dunloe, which is supposed to be only a walking route and a horse drawn jaunting route, but there were motorised vehicles travelling on the route as well. And sure enough, it was a step back in time. We knew it was roughly six miles one way and we decided that we wanted to go and see how far we were on the trip only to discover that all of our phones had no coverage.

In fact, one man pulled up in his car. Now I don't know what he was trying to do, but the next thing he went running up the road, then running up the rocks, halfway up the mountain looking for a signal and all I could think of was the guy on the ad in Jamaica, mobile phone to his ear shouting "Can you hear me now?" So that got me thinking about pilgrimage. Suddenly it was just us, the beautiful scenery, the road, and I mean it was just one road, there were no junctions either to the left or the right. It was literally just the only path you could travel on.

But there was time... time to talk, time to look at the scenery, time to look at the different things around us. As I said, it was a kind of pilgrimage of sorts. And so I got to thinking about Jacob and Pharaoh and their story, but also what is your story? what is my story?

I've been reading through the book of Revelation and am struck by those who survived the tribulation, who are the people whom God honoured as well. And the reason why is that they are those who have held fast to His word and their testimony of Jesus Christ. Their testimony is their story. Your testimony is your story.

And as I said I was thinking about Pharaoh and Jacob and a couple of verses that intrigued me in Genesis 47. This is Jacob at the end of his life and Pharaoh says, so what age are you? Jacob's response is very interesting. Jacob says in Genesis 47:9

> The years of my pilgrimage are 130. My years have been few and difficult and they do not equal the years of the pilgrimage of my fathers.

And then verse 10 tells us that Jacob went on to bless Pharaoh and left his presence. Tell me this, is that your story?

Chapter after chapter in the book of Genesis tell about Jacob and his life and what he was doing and how God was there for him. How God met him at Bethel. How the angels were going up and down that ladder and how it was that he decided to give God 10% of all he had if God were to bless him. But also how God did bless him, even though he had been codded and robbed. Yes, God still blessed him with all of his possessions and his sheep and everything else he acquired. God blessed him with two wives.

If you want to get into all that story you can find out about it for yourself. I personally think one wife is enough for any man! And yet with all that testimony of God's blessing, when Pharaoh asks him what age he was, he says, 'the years of my pilgrimage have been 130 and they have been few and difficult.' Now let me ask you a question: when you look back over your life, however long or short that may be, how do you see it? What testimony would you give? What is your story?

A pilgrimage frequently involves a journey or a search for moral or spiritual significance. So how has your journey been of moral or spiritual significance? How has your search been going? Are you someone who like Jacob, would say that the years of my pilgrimage have been few and difficult? Even though he's 130 years of age? I find that very negative, very depressing really. Why didn't Jacob just go and say to Pharaoh, I'm 130 years old and leave it at that? Or why didn't he add that his journey was a pilgrimage, or that his life had been a pilgrimage, or that it's been a journey of spiritual significance. But to add that his years had been few and difficult. That is hardly glorifying to God for all that God had brought him through, and most of it of his own making as well!

Anyway we got to the end of our journey through the Gap

of Dunloe, but on our little walk, I stumbled, I fell. Thankfully I didn't do much damage. I had just stepped off the road for one of the motorized vehicles going along and I slipped and bang, down I went, much to the mortification of myself and everybody else with me. But as we walked that journey, on the way it was all sunshine and then on our return journey we walked through the rain and the clouds.

Even though it was lovely, there was that real sense of adventure, sense of wonder and sense of oneness with all creation around us. There was also that sense of God's magnificence in it all.

Now you could decide to just focus in on the walk and sure the walk was one with a degree of difficulty. It was very up and down as you traversed the mountains. On the other hand, you could choose to focus in on the journey and relish the blessings that are contained within that journey.

So as you enjoy your 'an cupán tae,' let me ask you a very simple question. Are you someone who relishes the excitement of the journey, knowing that you can look back, and even though it's been difficult, even though it has been hard, even though there have been tough times, you know that it has been a blessed journey because God has been with you?

Are you the type of person who knows that your journey is full of absolutely amazing facts, adventures and stories of God's goodness contained within it? Or are you someone who can only see the difficulties and the hardships, and when you look back over everything the years of life have just been few and difficult!?

My prayer is that when you look back, when you reminisce on your pilgrimage, on your journey, it's one that excites you, it's one that fires you and enthuses you for what may lie ahead? Something for you to think about. A Pilgrimage frequently involves a journey or a search for moral or spiritual significance. I just want to say that I believe that significance can only be found in Jesus. I hope you'll be more aware of the environment on your next walk – you'll have a story to tell at the end of it

August 5th 2021

A Soft Day!

'Tis a soft day, thank God! Ah yeah, the ould rain is falling and so now 'tis a soft day! That's what we say here: 'Tis a soft day thank God!' It's a nice warm, gentle rain. And it's good to be with you for this 'an cupán tae' and to have a conversation. I got a little gift, I got a little present and it is class! A big thank you to Rebecca for this lovely coaster that says, 'Ewe and me and a cup of tea.' Plus there are two cups with sheep on them that also say 'Ewe and me' too. Ah that is brilliant. I love that.

Anyway, today seeing as it's raining, I was just thinking about this verse of scripture that I use in nearly every church service. And that is:

> Just as the rain falls from the sky and replenishes the earth before it returns, so too, the word of God does not return to him void, but accomplishes what He desires

It's from Isaiah 55:10-11. Just as the rain falls from the heavens and replenishes the earth before it returns, so too, the word of God does not return to him void. I love that. Do you know that that means every time that a verse of Scripture is read it will accomplish what God intended. I think this is mind-boggling. That is amazing!

Every time, I mean, every time a scripture is read, every time it is meditated on, every time that it is declared from a church pulpit, every time it's on the back of a bus, every time you see it on a poster, or anything like that, God's word accomplishes what God desires. That is fascinating.

It doesn't need a big, lengthy exhortation by me. It doesn't need us delving into it for hours though there's room for that. There is a need for us to be studying the word and getting stuck into the Bible and seeing what it says.

If you profess to be a Christian and you're not reading the Bible, that's basically like saying that you're a human being, but you don't need food, and so you don't go to the shop. I mean that's madness. But I just love that whole concept, that just as the rain falls on the earth and replenishes it, the Bible will replenish our souls.

Now, you know, being a small farmer, I am very happy to see a small bit of rain myself. It's causing the grass to grow, keeps the old cows fed, stuff like that. And everyone is going, oh yeah, typical of the farmers, they are never happy. But I was very happy when it was nice and warm, it was lovely you know. But I'm equally very happy to see the rain because the old grass is getting burnt into the ground, and how! So now it's going to be replenished just as the rain falls from the heavens and replenishes the earth.

When you go out there in the warmth and the heat, you'll actually see the grass jumping out of your ground. You know, your lawn will bloom. You know, it's amazing. The flowers open up. And blossom. Even at this point in the autumn, as things are starting to die back, there's still that fresh flurry of life and growth with rain.

So, I just decided that today I'm going to do something very simple. Today I'm just going to read a little bit of Scripture, but this is God's invitation to you. I'm not going to say anything about it. I'm not going to speak on it. After all, God says His word is just as the rain that falls, and so His word accomplishes what He desires. So what is God's desire in your life today as you read this? That's between you and God. Or if you want to share with someone, please share it. But listen to this. This is God speaking to you through the scripture in Isaiah 55:1-3a:

> Come, all you who are thirsty. Come to the waters. Come, buy and eat. Come, buy wine and milk without money and without cost. Why spend money on what is not bread? And your labour on what does not satisfy? Listen, listen to me and eat what is good. And your soul will delight in the richest of fare. Give ear and come to me. Hear me. That your soul may live.

As I said, I'm not going to make any comment, guys. It's God's word. So, thank you for joining me with this 'an cupán tae.' If you ever have a chance, let me know what God has been saying to you. Until next time, the Lord bless and let us rejoice in the joy of a soft day.

August 12th 2021

The Rev's Philosophy About an Apple Tree

How's it going? Welcome to our 'an cupán tae with the Rev.' As you can see I'm outside and today I want to talk to you about 'Nigel's philosophy' of the apple tree. Some of you may have heard this before but here's our apple tree and it's laden down with apples. And the point I want to bring out to you is this, that very often in life when we are going through difficulties and hardships we find ourselves under pressure.

This apple tree right now is under pressure because it is laden with fruit and so it's straining just trying to keep itself upright. It is at this time that apple trees break with the weight that they are under. So my poor apple tree is laden down here with fruit and, trust me, it's under serious stress, and strain.

When it's spring it's not under any strain because it's only starting out on its annual journey when the buds are starting to come out. It's not under strain during the summer because it's only starting to come into leaves, and then the blossoms come out on it and the apples are only starting to form. But here in the autumn, the tree is looking awesome when the apples are at their fullest despite being weighed down, under strain, under pressure.

This tree is struggling right now. It's at breaking point. But here's the thing, it's at that point that it is the most fruitful. The apple tree doesn't know that it's at breaking point but it is, it's at breaking point. The scripture that this reminds me of is James 1:2-4:

> Consider pure joy my brethren. Whenever you face trials of many kinds. And here's why. Because you know that the testing of your faith develops perseverance. And perseverance must finish its work so that you may be mature and complete, not lacking anything.

So here's this apple tree. And it is struggling under the weight. But the thing is, the apple tree can't see the fruit. And very often when we're going through hardship and trial and difficult situations, let's be honest, the last thing we're thinking of is it being pure joy! The last thing we're thinking of is this is a time to party! The thought we are wrestling with is I'm going through hardship. So when James says consider it pure joy when you face many hardships and trials, it doesn't sit easy, does it.

However, what I'm saying is, what is God actually doing in you? What is the fruit that other people are seeing? What is the fruit that God is seeing in your life when you're going through that difficult situation. Right now your faith is being developed. Faith develops perseverance. And perseverance must finish its work which is bringing us to maturity in Christ. So all I want to say on this little 'an cupán tae', is if you're going through a situation in your life right now, and you're feeling weighed down, if you're feeling that you just can't cope with the pressures of life and you're feeling that your branches are about to break, you're feeling that you just might keel over and you're feeling that you just might snap right now, just like the apple tree… Hold on. Stand firm. This is a time of growth. God is building you up.

Others may see the fruit of what God is doing in your life. You may not feel it right now. You might even know the presence of God right now. The apple tree is just doing its best to stand up right now. It's not thinking about the fruit. But I'm the beneficiary of the fruit. And anyone who comes and takes from that tree is the beneficiary of the fruit.

So let me ask you a question. Even though you're really going through this rubbish experience, through this difficult time, through hardship: do you consider it pure joy? Knowing that God may be revealing His character to others through you. After all the Spirit of God lives within you.

And the fruit of the Spirit. What are they? Galatians chapter 5. I'm going to read it here really quickly, just to remind you.

Part of the reason I want to read it is because I know that even though I could try to say them all, I'm going to forget one or two of them. Because my forgetery is getting more forgetery all the time. Okay, to the fruit of the Spirit, Galatians 5:22-23:

> But the fruit of the Spirit. is love, joy, peace, patience, kindness, goodness, faithfulness, gentleness and self-control.

So even though you can't see what fruit others are seeing in your life? You probably don't know others the answer. You'll probably never know the answer. But God does. So even though you're under the cosh, even though you're in this time of trial, whatever your trial may be, here's the thing, even in that time of trial, remember this, consider it pure joy. Why? Because your faith develops perseverance. Let's not give up. Let's keep ploughing on.

August 19th 2021

All Fenced In!

Ohhh! I have him fenced in, boy he is fenced in! Welcome to 'an cupán tae with the Rev.' Yes, there we go. At last we have that Rooster the right side of the wire. I think I'll call him John, seeing as the other fellow is already called Peter As you know, John was there at the time when the cock crowed twice. Yes, John was there when Peter went and denied Jesus three times before the cock crew twice. So I think we'll call this fellow after John. So Peter and John were outside their fence for a minute.

Oh, folks, I tell you what, the thing is that I've been building the fence, as I said, Queen Victoria has a big renovation plan going on, and so we had to go and sort the whole thing out. And here we are looking at a grand new fence. But now that I've told you about the fence, and spoken about John the cockerel there I just want to talk to you over this passage of scripture in Hebrews. In fact, I'll read it to you as it's about being fenced in. And I think this is interesting stuff. I'm reading it from Hebrew 6:13-20 and this is what it says:

"When God made his promise to Abraham, since there was no one greater for him to swear by, he swore by himself, saying, I will surely bless you and give you many descendants. And so after waiting patiently, Abraham received what was promised. Now, people swear by someone greater than themselves. And the oath confirms what he said and puts an end to all argument. Because God wanted to make His unchangeable purpose very clear to the heirs of promise, He confirmed it with an oath. And God did this by two unchangeable things in which it is impossible for God to lie. We who have fled to take hold of the hope offered to us may be greatly encouraged, because we have a hope as an anchor for the soul, firm and secure. It enters the inner sanctuary behind the curtain, where Jesus who went before us, has entered on our behalf"

So there you go. Now, the thing is, what on earth has that passage got to do with fencing? Well, now that we have the old fencing done, here is what it means. It says in that passage of Scripture that people go and swear by someone greater than themselves.

Do you know how many times you have ended up in a discussion, or an argument starts to come about and then someone says, 'I swear on my mother's life', or 'I swear on my mother's grave'. I don't know why they want to do that, to be honest. I think it's a bit daft. My mother's alive and well, and to be honest with you, I don't want to be swearing on her life. And I definitely don't want to be swearing on her grave. But people say that sort of stuff. They go and swear by something greater than themselves is what that Scripture says.

And so because God couldn't swear... Now, that's interesting, isn't it? So because God couldn't swear by anything greater than himself, He took an oath. Now, here's what it is that really excited me the first time I read this. The word oath means to 'fence oneself in'. The Greek word for it is 'horkos' and it literally translates as 'to fence oneself in'. So what it's actually saying is that God has fenced himself in to fulfilling the promise.

So here we are, and we're making a fence outside, and we're keeping in Peter and John and all the rest of the poultry behind it so that when Queen Victoria drives in, she can look out at her lovely chickens and go, "Don't they look beautiful!" Really? Well I have other opinions about that, but we'll talk about that another day. So here's the thing, that term "fenced in" excites me no end, because stop and think about it. I have been sharing with you through this little 'an cupán tae' many times about how God has gone and has promised us different things such as the fact that He never leaves us nor forsakes us, or that He will always be with us, or that He promises to hold us in the palm of His hand, or that no one can snatch us out of the palm of His hand, or that we have been given eternal life through the person of Jesus Christ, or that God has shown, demonstrated His love for us, because while we were yet sinners Christ died for us… All these promises given to us through Christ, what a privilege!

But with all these promises, now just think about this, God has fenced himself in to fulfilling these promises in our lives. God has contained all of Himself, poured all of Himself into fulfilling His promise to you. Just pause and think about that. Digging back into the text it tells us that it's impossible for God to lie, and that he made this promise to Abraham, but He has made those promises to you, and God has fenced Himself in to fulfil them.

So just as we've gone and stuck up the old fence there to keep Peter and John in the other side, we won't be able to stop them crowing and making a racket, that's a different problem. But the thing is this, the fence will keep them in that area, their new chicken run has been built. And they have been contained.

In the same capacity God has literally put a fence around Himself, He has fenced Himself into fulfilling His word in your life. So what promises do you hold on to? What promises have you read in this Bible where you can go and say, Lord, this is your word…

Now, it's not that you're holding God over a barrel, or anything, but God must honour His word. God has fenced Himself in to fulfilling His word in your life. So when God's word states for example in one of the first 'an cupán taes' we ever shared where it says, 'if you delight yourself in the Lord, He will give you the desire of your heart' from Psalm 37:4 - that verse has a promise. The promise is that if you delight in Him, He will give you the desire of your heart. Scripture also tells us that if you believe in Him, He will give you eternal life. He has promised never to leave you nor forsake you. He has fenced Himself into fulfilling these promises. There is no 'get-out clause' with or for God.

God, imagine it my friend, the whole majesty of God, the magnificence of God, the awesomeness of God, the holiness of God, the goodness of God, the love of God, all of God fenced into fulfilling His promise to you. So what promise have you got? What has God promised you?

Until next week, may the Lord bless you and keep you. Thanks for joining me for this 'an cupán tae' and, man, am I buzzing and I pray you are too.

August 26th 2021

A Beautiful Story.

Well, welcome to our 'an cupán tae with the Rev.' This week I was having a chat with a few people and I was just thinking on things, I was actually sharing a song that I had written and these are the lyrics of that song:

> I am that lonely kid,
> who never made the grade,
> always failed, standards I and others made.
> I am that child from the dying rooms
> where Satan is the master and Death he
> calls the tunes.

Back in the last millennium there was a documentary called "The Dying Rooms" and it made a big furore at the time, but it's amazing the number of people that I have spoken to that have no recollection of it. That documentary really impacted my life. I don't know, I would go and say it was possibly life-changing for me.

But it also gave me a life changing understanding of the gospel, a life-changing understanding of God's good news, and at the start of this year I was sharing about how this is the year of the Lord's favour and that we have been anointed to preach good news. If you are a Christian, it doesn't matter what tradition you are, if you are someone who professes to know Jesus Christ as your Lord and Saviour, you have got good news - hope, peace, love, joy, the presence of God, the assurance of God. That's all good news that you can bring into your environment.

As I said, irrespective of what tradition you come from, if you profess to be a Christian, a follower of Christ, you carry good news.

But this documentary really impacted my life and another thing that really impacted my life, and at this point, Queen Victoria and I were married, and we went to the Czech Republic and visited an orphanage and we met a little girl. This was 20 years ago, exactly this year. We met a little girl called Maria, who was three at the time. Maria is someone who has really, I don't know, found a place in my spirit. I think of her often.

But anyway, she was someone we were told who was never going to be adopted. She was someone who was never going to find a home because of the colour of her skin, because of her background. That's what we were told, just to put us straight. And she was three at the time. There was nothing we could do. We were helpless in the situation. There was no way we were going to be able to help her and I have often thought about her and prayed about her since. I mean often.

That was over 20 years ago but as I said 'The Dying Rooms' really impacted my life. The dying rooms was an orphanage of sorts for unwanted babies.

But the thing was, it was literally called that because if as a baby you could feed yourself, you lived. If you couldn't, you didn't. It was so understaffed that the poor women who were trying to look after all these babies went along with their shopping trolley and were just literally throwing the bottle of milk into the cots and everything. It was just horrendous. The thing was, because of the law that you could have only one child, it meant those extra children were discarded.

It made no difference what religion they were. It made no difference what theology it was. It made no difference what their background was. It made no difference, they were just placed in this dying room and left to die and it impacted me greatly.

I was one of these 'weird and wonderful folk' when I was in college. I used to wear a long black morning coat, a bowler hat, dark jeans and I was lying back in a couch, you know, feet up, looking at the television, dressed like that with tears just rolling down my face. And you know it gave me a picture of God, it really did. In the Bible, in Romans 8:15 -16 it says:

> For all who are led by the Spirit of God are children of God, for you did not receive a spirit of slavery to fall back into fear but you have received a spirit of adoption. When we cry Abba Father, it is the very Spirit bearing witness with our spirit that we are children of God and if children then heirs, heirs of God and joint heirs with Christ, if in fact we suffer with Him so that we may also be glorified with Him.

If you have gone through an adoption process or you have adopted someone, it is all about the giver, and God is like that. God has entered into our world, into the dying rooms of this world and there is a procedure. In Ephesians 2:1-2 it says that we belong to the Prince of this world, we were under Satan's rule in the dying rooms so to speak and as I stated in my song 'I am that child from the dying rooms where Satan is the master and death he calls the tunes". Now you may say that is a very fatalistic view of the world but it is the truth.

But then Jesus stepped in, as many people did after that documentary; before China closed its doors. Then Jesus stepped into our dying room and He paid the ransom. He paid for our adoption with his blood. Every adoption procedure costs money, whether you like it or not. And Jesus came and he took me, took you out of that dying room after paying the price so that we could go and benefit from being part of his family. We can now be children of God. It is a beautiful picture. God was so moved with compassion, so moved by His love that He had to intervene.

If you look at the outcry, the outpouring of love and compassion that took place at the time of 'The Dying

Rooms', you can see that people were so motivated that they had to go and interact, they had to do something. And God, in our case, He had to do something. In regard to the people of Israel, God said, when he called Moses to liberate the people of Israel 'I have heard my people's cry'. In Exodus 3:7.

So God stepped in with love and compassion. God paid for my adoption in his blood. God went and brought me into his presence. God sent Jesus so that I could be a part of his family. I am just as much a part of God's family as Jesus Christ is because I have been adopted into the family.

And it is the same for you, if you know Jesus Christ as your Lord and Saviour. If you profess to be a Christian, then this is what God has done for you. It is for freedom that Christ has set us free.

I know this is heavy, it is reflective, but as I said, folks, it just breaks my heart to think that someone like Maria was out there with no hope. It breaks my heart to think that there are people out there in our world right now, and they have come to a point where they believe that there is no hope, when there is hope in Christ. He has paid the price. The adoption papers are sealed. The Spirit of God is within us, guaranteeing our inheritance. It is good news, good news! We are liberated from the dying rooms. It is a beautiful story. That documentary still impacts my life and I pray that this 'an cupán tae' impacts you… God bless!

Printed in Dunstable, United Kingdom

68562932R00118